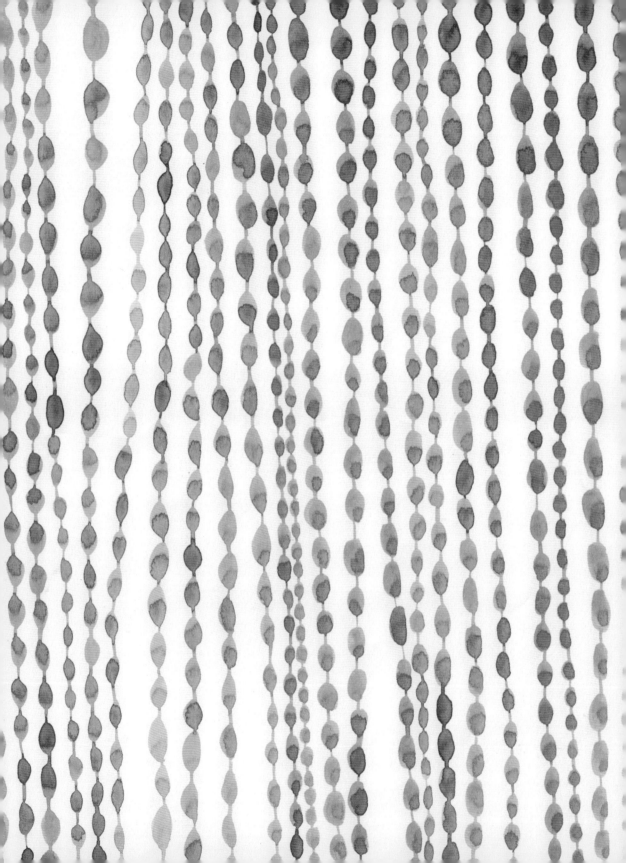

Beyond Widow

INSPIRATION FROM THE TRENCHES

For Keith and Richard

Beyond Widow

INSPIRATION FROM THE TRENCHES

Patty McGuigan *and* Tesha McCord Poe
with Marian Lye

Illustrations Priska Wenger Mage
Cartoons John Klossner

Introduction.

Becoming a widow can feel like a fall into a deep trench, a place where it is difficult to see above the edge, and where it's hard to even imagine new possibilities for a changed life. Even under the best circumstances, navigating the route from survival to feeling good again is one of the hardest journeys a woman can make. At the time of writing, 11.4 million women in the U.S. are on that journey of widowhood, trying to find their path to a new chapter in their lives. We, and perhaps you, or maybe someone you know, are numbered among them.

We two authors, Patty and Tesha, had known each other through business before widowhood challenged each of us to reshape our lives in a world changed by loss and the COVID-19 pandemic. We are from different backgrounds; Patty was working in commercial real estate and beginning to write children's books,

while Tesha was starting Joy-Raising, a consulting business to guide folks in philanthropy.

After we became widows, during a lunch date, we swapped stories of poignant, painful, and sometimes funny moments we had been through as widows. The more we talked, the more we realized what a void there is around this subject in society. Growing up we aren't given the tools to talk about grief and death, which can make it even harder to face when it becomes a part of your own life.

Tesha brought up a time when she picked up a book on grief, only to feel a quick panic at not being even remotely able to commit to the roller coaster of emotions it seemed to require. As we were discussing this, that's when we decided there needed to be something else! A book that would speak to our truths and experiences from the trenches of widowhood, from our two distinct perspectives.

Our hope was to write a book that would pull no punches, that could assist you to negotiate your way through your kingdom of grief and help you to imagine a new chapter for yourself. A book that would help open up conversations about a topic that can be hard to discuss or can make folks feel very alone. A beautiful

"dip into" book, where you don't have to start at the first page and work your way through to the end. But something to keep on your bedside table or bring along in your purse for needed reminders and encouragement.

So curl up with a cup of tea or a glass of wine and start somewhere, wherever you are. We hope that these pages will bring you some solace, inspire confidence or comfort you like a warm hug. And maybe our stories can even introduce a new idea or challenge to you, like the two of us did for each other as we laughed and cried over our experiences as widows that day.

Patty & Tesha

Table of Contents.

Pure Survival

Start where you are.
Use what you have.
Do what you can.

—Arthur Ashe

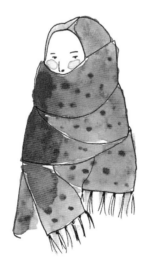

The difference a day makes.

Patty

Yesterday, you were married. You and your spouse probably spent many years together, creating a home, working, raising a family, sharing time and memories. Today, you've woken up and everything is changed. Today you are a widow.

Maybe this day has come about after a long illness experienced by your spouse, or perhaps it has happened very suddenly. Either way, you are exhausted, shocked and feeling numb. However, there's an initial tsunami of necessary things to sort out and arrangements to be made, all of which occupy your immediate time and effort. To some extent, being carried along on that wave blunts the reality for a short while, and family and friends around you can help to cushion the blow, but one way or another, the realization starts to sink in… your other half has gone. Life as you knew it is over!

Immediately after your loss, you may just want to hide away, catlike, to lick your wounds. If you have young children and you're now the sole breadwinner, you don't have the luxury to do that. You need to come out of your bedroom and start fighting, even if you're on autopilot for a while. Similarly, if you're older, but not sure of financial provision, you may need to reexamine your finances and your new way of life. Gradually, as you get this next phase sorted, there will be moments to smile and reflect upon the good memories. And there will be moments where you sob pushing the shopping cart in front of you. You'll come to realize that solitude does not always equate to loneliness. And that it's possible to feel sad and happy at the very same time.

In the words of a Beatles' song – *Let it be.*

My first responder is gone.

Tesha

Even if we were too upset with each other to share a bed, I never ever doubted that, if a strange bump came in the night, I could rely on Keith to be our first responder. He was a big man who did brave things, and we never debated that he would get up first. Perhaps this is why he slept lightly, like a watchdog, and from time to time awoke with a startle as if he was escaping from a dangerous nightmare adventure. My first responder is gone, and so sleep comes to me less peacefully.

Celebrating a life.

Patty

After a death, there comes something we now call the celebration of life. Right on the heels of losing your partner, you are expected to plan a party. I was numb. I did not write an obituary. I was simply incapable of capturing Richard in words. But I knew I could not escape holding this celebratory event. I remembered Steve Jobs's words: "Think different." Well, that's me… I think different. I wanted to celebrate Richard, and I was not going to have people stand up and talk about what they thought of him while we all teared up.

So I gave birth to a special celebration… it would be a musical entitled "Hats off to Richard!" And that's what we did. We had a playbill printed with the lyrics and fun pictures of Dick. We had a DJ and everyone sang and danced. I gathered nine songs that told his story. And I enlisted people who had been engaged in all different parts of Richard's life to get up and sing those songs. We all joined in and it was brilliant! And so a tiny bit of closure had begun.

Waking up under water.

Tesha

There's this feeling that I had after Keith died. I had the same feeling when my dad was diagnosed with stage 4 cancer less than a year before Keith passed. In just a few months my dad rapidly declined and succumbed to his third cancer battle. In some ways, that feeling while Dad was sick was even worse than after he was gone, because I didn't know what the night had brought or what the day would deliver. I'd wake up and for a short moment I wouldn't remember. Then, like waking up under water in a deep ocean, I would gasp and take in all of the suffocating weight of the moment I was in. The one that couldn't be avoided when I was fully awake. And rather than fight, I would drown in the realization that my life was different now. And that it would never be the same again. Day after day, I would wake up to this. A brief moment of reprieve and then that underwater drowning in feelings that surrounded me and gave me no possible escape. For weeks and maybe months, I avoided going to sleep, perhaps trying to permanently delay this incessant morning routine. Perhaps this is what it means to be in crisis.

But one morning, nearly a year since Keith had been gone, I woke up and his death wasn't my first thought, and when I thought of him, I didn't panic. I didn't drown under the weight of the inescapable. I don't know when that changed or which stage of grief that puts me in. But I do know that I'm ready to get up and face another day.

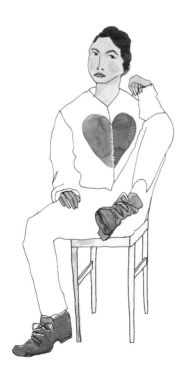

There is no such thing as a young widow.

Tesha

The truth is that there is no such thing as a young widow because being a widow ages you. I've been forced to grow up and face issues that I'd planned to put off for decades. It feels like what's left of my youth has been snatched away at a time when I need it most in order to have a chance to survive. I won't possibly be attractive to someone else if I no longer believe that I'm beautiful. I must live with a measure of unfettered optimism in order to have the where-withal to learn all of the new things that are required of me in order to survive. I feel like a lion cub in a world where I have the potential to grow to be a king; but right now, I am prey. I silently panic that, with one wrong move, I will be whisked away into a state of irrelevance from which I cannot escape. I choose to hold tight to believing that there is something left for me to offer. Right? Because living my remaining days only as a receptacle of periodic acts of good-will is not enough motivation to make all of this effort to counter these head-winds.

With a little more time, I can make a dent in this world.

The world needs a new condolence sentence.

Patty

People keep saying, "Sorry for your loss." But they don't really know what that means and, frankly, neither do you.

"What can I do?" is another one. But these expressions seldom lead to meaningful exchanges. I've learned that offering a warm smile and saying to a widow, "How is your life evolving?" is a much more positive and thoughtful invitation to open a real conversation!

What would you like to hear instead?

Pity is not useful.

Tesha

"It's the thought that counts." But what if that thought is rooted in pity and comes from a sense of superiority? Death is awkward, and I don't think there's a way to always avoid dumb and insensitive comments. They're bound to show up. And because that is true, I want permission to reply to insensitive talk with clarity and without apology.

Instead, regardless of any lack of social grace in delivery or content, it feels like I am expected to just be grateful for someone else's interest in my situation, even if what has been done or said feels pretty awful. Of course, this is only a small percentage of the gestures that have come my way in a sea of beautiful sharing and connection that has kept me afloat.

But still, not every interaction that has been presented as concern has felt like a gift. No matter how bad things are, no one wants to feel like they are a charity. Believe this and please act accordingly. Still wondering what I mean? Consider this: if you say to someone, "I can't imagine what it would be like to be in your shoes," then you're also declaring that you don't have to. Instead you can ask yourself, "If I were in this situation, what would I need?" It's a slight shift, but instead of shoring up the difference in our circumstances, you've provided the gift of a willingness to take my pain for a moment. That is in fact the gift.

Wonder Widows

Inspiration from the past by Marian Lye

The word "widow" can have a somber, hushed association. But we know that widowhood is just one part of a person's identity, not its defining factor. As we explored the topic, we marveled over stories of widows that reflect incredible hope and empowerment through how they continued to lead their lives. So much to the contrary from how widows are often publicly portrayed in most societies, these women have achieved quite wondrous things.

It is important however, for you to remember that we are not trying to hold up these women as role models for what a widow "should" be or do. Rather, we seek to illustrate, through them, that after great loss, completely new chapters of life can still lay ahead of you.

You don't have to take on a huge project. Your moment of beginning a new path can start as simply as deciding to organize your closet in a different way than you did as a married person. No matter how small your decisions may be, they should be about what makes you feel good and brings you a sense of joy.

Whether it is just getting out of bed in the morning or pursuing a new career path, we aim to inspire you with chapters ahead filled with hope and curiosity, even while you are living with grief.

The vibrant community of widows we've found includes the following:

Madame Clicquot

A widow who built a luxury brand that is still relevant today

Barbe-Nicole Ponsardin, who became Madame Clicquot, lived from 1777 to 1866 and created Veuve Clicquot (widow Clicquot), the world-famous French champagne brand. She was born in Reims to wealthy parents who ensured their daughter received a good education. During the French Revolution, Barbe-Nicole was married at twenty-one years of age to François Clicquot, whose family had a small winery. At twenty-seven, when her husband died in a typhoid epidemic, she became a widow with a young daughter to care for.

Barbe-Nicole was now at a crossroads in her life, but she was not about to retreat into the shadows of widowhood. She decided to take over the winery and turn it into a success. However, in a male-dominated society, everything was against her; women were not seen as being able to run a business, and her father-in-law was adamant that he would close the winery. But Barbe-Nicole won him over and he agreed that she could continue… if he could choose a male business partner to work with her.

Her first steps into the world of winemaking faltered. Cultivating and selling her product in a Europe beset by wars was no easy task; demand dwindled and debts piled up. In 1810, her business partner ended the agreement to work together. Barbe-Nicole was pressured again by her father-in-law to close the winery. Undaunted, she worked to develop a quality product using a technique called riddling, which resulted in a clear, sparkling champagne. Barbe-Nicole also added her maiden name to the company's title to rebrand the business.

The Clicquot-Ponsardin winery flourished and was soon selling the first vintage champagne. Acclaim for the champagne grew far and wide. Napoleon called for her champagne to celebrate his victories—or to console himself when he lost a battle. While war continued in Europe, Barbe-Nicole gave Napoleon's officers champagne in return for protection for her land and she captured the market in Russia, where Tsar Alexander I stated that her champagne was his favorite. Today, Veuve Clicquot is in demand everywhere and asking for a "widow" ensures the delivery of a bottle of top-shelf champagne bearing Barbe-Nicole's trademark yellow label.

Years after her feats as a businesswoman, Barbe-Nicole's advice to her granddaughter was to act boldly! Despite prejudice against women and a series of wars, this resourceful widow created one of the greatest champagne houses in the world. Her legacy continues through BOLD, Veuve Clicquot's foundation which celebrates bold and inspirational women worldwide.

The salute.

Tesha

The service is the crescendo. You know it will not last.
That these grieving people will go. And then what will your life be?
They are a moment of truth. A grace. A passage.

We stood for three hours. Masked against COVID-19. With pretty dresses,
freshly done hair. It was important to me that we represent Keith well.
That his people could see that he provided for us and that we were beautiful
and strong.

All of these things are true, but it was important for them to be undeniably true.
It seemed like an act of respect.

The widow emergency room.

Patty

Carve out a physical space that you can have just for yourself when overwhelming moments come. When the school calls, a nasty bill arrives, the toilet is clogged up, or you're unexpectedly out of milk. These moments will come suddenly and they just crash down on you.

This is when you need the Widow Emergency Room, a space set up with the things that comfort you and make you feel safe. And this doesn't have to be a separate room. It can be a corner somewhere or a favorite armchair. Settle yourself into your space, close your eyes, breathe deeply, and transport yourself to a heavenly spot. Have the things that make you feel good at hand. For me, that's lipstick, perfume, and a hairbrush; but for you, it might be something totally different. You may want to hold on to something, light a candle, look at a photo that warms your heart, or listen to your favorite music.

Tell yourself: "I am safe, I am loved, and whatever I am feeling right now, it's okay." Repeat this to yourself as often as you need it. And when you are ready, stand up, stretch, and face your day!

The ten widow commandments.

Patty

1. GIVE YOURSELF PERMISSION to experience joy again

It's OK to shed a tear. You're human! We all experience everything from joy to sadness and sometimes all at once. When bereavement happens, it's good to cry and feel the feels. BUT don't let grief consume you to the detriment of all else. Prolonged grief will damage your physical and mental health. Seek help if you need it and accept that it's time to take care of your own well-being, especially if you were the carer for your spouse. Self-care includes allowing yourself to experience joy again.

2. SAY YES to connections with people!

We all need each other, so keep in touch with friends and your community. Make technology your friend. Use social media and email to exchange photos and news and build a new community for yourself.

3. RAISE YOUR HAND for opportunities and adventures!

Look outwards again and step up to new adventures, whether it's taking a class or starting a new hobby. Learn to play golf, tennis, or another sport, or volunteer in your community. This will keep you meeting other people and having new experiences.

4. LOVE YOUR BODY. Your health is your focus. Take care of it!

Your health is vital to making the most of the next phase in your life. Don't neglect your physical or mental health! Group fitness classes provide a healthy activity, plus new people to meet. Exercise with a pal.

5. BUILD a new routine

Instead of following the same old routines, build some new ones! You're in charge of these, not the other way around. Have something on your calendar to get you out of the house, and walk every day, preferably in different directions.

6. MAKE YOUR BED

Making your bed at the start of the day is a good way to reinforce the fact that you are beginning a fresh, new twenty-four hours. And if your day was horrible, at least you come back to a nicely made bed!

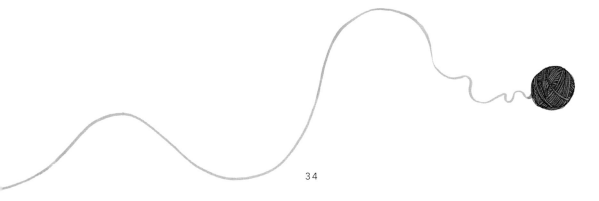

7. FIND A WAY TO EAT BY YOURSELF that is pleasant

Make eating by yourself more of an adventure! When I don't feel like cooking an elaborate meal, I go for what I feel like—even if it's popcorn with a glass of wine. Your meals can be what you want and when you want them. But try different things until you find a way to fuel yourself in a way that feels good to you.

8. TURN THE HOUSE AROUND

Turning "our house" into "my house" can be liberating! Your home can work the way you want. No need to compromise now over color schemes, room arrangements, furnishings, or anything else. Keep what you really like, but if you want a red ceiling or a zebra-striped sofa, why not?

9. REIMAGINE what is possible

It's never too late to start a new career or pursue your talents. If you have children, it's not fair to expect them to fill your void. That can be a recipe for disaster! They have a right to live their own lives. Don't cast aside the chance to discover a new life for yourself, with new opportunities for fulfillment!

10. WEAR SOMETHING RED

Red is the color of courage. A tiny dash goes a long way! Even if it's just a bright lipstick, a small piece of jewelry, a scarf or your purse, red is your badge of courage to brave the world. There's no better example of this than Queen Elizabeth II of Great Britain, whose husband of seventy-three years, Prince Philip, died in April 2021. At his funeral service, which was socially distanced because of COVID-19, she sat alone. Eight months later, delivering her annual Christmas message on TV, she was the epitome of courage and determination… in her red dress!

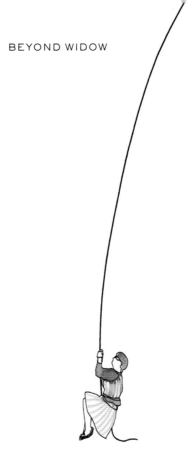

When you are at the end of your rope,
tie a knot in it and hold on.

—Theodore Roosevelt

Don't bring the darkness.

Tesha

Here's the scenario that keeps repeating. I face a moment where I must choose to act or risk falling into darkness. My fear is of a darkness that attaches like molasses or maybe like tar. A dark and heavy substance that becomes impossible to escape if I sit in it too long. I'm running from this darkness. I'm earnestly trying to manage it. To stay afloat. Well, better than that. To thrive. That's what this writing is about, saving myself and hopefully providing a tool to help others to do the same.

The darkness is always there. I wonder if it always will be. Will it be diluted with time, new habits, and enough new memories? Will it feel less like a weight and more like a layer of clothing? A comfortable armor in my new world?

I wish that I had more cultural guidance for how I should behave. No wonder people are marveling at my strength. I didn't know that I was supposed to mourn in private and reemerge at some unspoken time with a brave smile. Instead, I live out loud and I invite witnesses and community into my process. "Yes, it is as awful as you can imagine," I say often. But it is not only that. It is also beautiful to witness the most stunning demonstrations of support that humans can offer.

A widow-in-waiting

Patty

A widow-in-waiting is a woman who suffers an ambiguous loss over an extended period. As a widow-in-waiting, it might be clear that your spouse is dying, and the life you knew together is not the same anymore. If he is suffering from mental decay, you might feel like his spirit has already left. You can't mourn his passing because he is still physically here. It can be a long goodbye and the kind of limbo that makes a woman feel like a widow-in-waiting.

We are all going to die one day, but talking about death is a taboo subject in many cultures. If your spouse receives news of a terminal condition, accepting that diagnosis takes courage on both sides. Having a conversation on the subject (sooner rather than later) can be hugely difficult, but it can also be liberating and make it easier to plan and prepare together for what the future will hold.

I have a friend who experienced the sadness of the long goodbye. Louise was thirty-four when she married Jack. She was ambitious and a truly delightful and kind person. Jack was fifty-four and they had a humble, good life. They did everything together—skiing, golfing, hunting—and they each made every effort to make life wonderful for the other.

Because Jack's mother had Alzheimer's and lived until she was ninety-two, Jack had a real fear of it, and at around sixty-two, he started showing signs of that disease himself. He slipped down that road for almost twenty years until he passed away at age eighty-six. Louise put aside a lot of her own needs and ambitions and traveled every step of that hard road with him. When he was in day care, and then later living in a facility, she went every day to see him, although he no longer knew who she was. She once told me she'd sit in the car, saying to herself, "I can't do this today…" but she did it anyway. At one point, she began to worry if their money would run out while Jack still needed care and what that would mean for her own life. It was a tough existence for her for over eighteen years. Louise may not have been a widow then, but she was a widow-in-waiting.

Louise has now been a widow for six years and still grieves for him. My friend Diane and I went to lunch with her a while back, when my husband was still alive. It was just after Louise became a "true" widow. Diane and I had been feeling sorry for ourselves, moaning about our own husbands' shortcomings and medical challenges, annoyances, etc. Louise looked up and said quietly: "If I had known when I was younger exactly what the future held, I would have done it all over again, just like it happened. We had such a love affair." I teared up, feeling selfish and heartless because it was so touching.

Each widow's loss takes its own form. Let's remember and include our sisters who are caring for their ailing spouses, sometimes for many years. If you know someone in this situation, reach out to them and show them that you see them, acknowledge them, and support them. If you need inspiration on how to do this, turn to our piece "How to support a widow" (see page 70) as the suggestions there can also apply to a widow-in-waiting. Each small act of kindness can go a very long way.

Grief will find you.

Patty

Grief is a hard thing to come to terms with. As Queen Elizabeth II famously said, "Grief is the price we pay for love." Just remind yourself that it is the measure of the strength of that love.

The Victorian era marked a time of obsession with mourning, and loss was lamented loudly and lasted long. Today, people often keep their thoughts and feelings about their loss more private, or try to keep a positive attitude. And perhaps we have swung the pendulum a little too far over to the other side. Our public expression of loss now takes the form of an acknowledgment and celebration of the life that was lived, instead of focusing on the pain of the loss.

However, grief and loss are parts of everyone's lives. Or as Queen Elizabeth also said, as a new widow during her Christmas Day broadcast in 2021, "Life consists of final partings as well as first meetings." She reminded us that life is a combination of grief and joy.

Or in my own words: Life is f***ing messy, and so are parts of widowhood! And those messy parts have to be named and dealt with. There is no escaping them.

If you can do that alone, that's perfectly fine. And if not, there is absolutely no shame in asking for professional help. Maintaining your mental health is just as vital as looking after your physical health. If managing grief gets too hard to bear, there are expert resources available.

(Find resources for dealing with grief on our website at beyondwidow.com)

The new three Rs.

Patty

There are three words beginning with the letter R which I kept in mind during the very early days of my widowhood: Resilience, Relevance and Reinvention! These three words helped me to move forward. For the reader who has suffered a loss, I offer this outlook and some words of advice:

RESILIENCE — Dig deep and find your resilience.

Resilience is the ability to recover from shock, sickness or hardship. It's about your confidence to be able to assess a situation or a problem and get to the other side. The artist Alicia Henry said: "There is always change. Whether it's big change or small change. It's about how you approach it, your openness to it." Some people possess great resilience or positivity, while others are easily overwhelmed and have to develop and practice this ability. If you find your resilience reservoir is low, find yourself a good therapist! Although support will doubtless be offered by family or close friends, they are also emotionally affected by your loss.

RELEVANCE — Stay relevant in your life and to the people around you.

This means keeping up with matters in hand and continuing to be a presence in things going on around you by not abdicating or becoming invisible. Relevance is a concept that becomes even more important as you grow older. You might feel that fewer people need you. It's easy to become very dull if you don't search for ways to connect to people who you can help and who can help you. Make it your focus to stay connected with friends, even if it's only by phone or email initially. Accept an invitation for coffee or dinner, then write it on your calendar and be sure to keep it. If you turn invitations down, people won't ask you again. Go out into the world. There's no time to be shy; walk and talk and ask questions! When I go to bed, I review my day and think about who I've met during those past hours.

REINVENTION — Dare to reinvent yourself.

Do you remember Halloween when you were a kid, and you thought of what character you wanted to be? Now do it in real life! Reinvention can be trying a new hairstyle or adding some fun jewelry to an outfit. Or maybe you begin by moving some furniture around or painting a wall a different color. "Widow" is just one letter away from "window." Allow yourself to look outwards again. Think about new things you might try, like a class, or rediscover activities that you've enjoyed in the past. I really believe in reinvention. I was a real estate agent raising kids and running a home. Here I am now, writing books, collaborating on a play, and riding my bike daily! Whatever you do doesn't have to be perfect, or even good. Just do it!

Get ready to live this next phase in your life. Even if it feels sometimes like you are taking three steps forward and two steps back, you ARE moving forward!

"YES, I'M HAVING CHOCOLATE CAKE FOR BREAKFAST. BECAUSE I CAN."

Songs for comfort.

Patty

Music is a powerful brain tool. It can give you energy and perspective, and connect you with your soul. You can use music to fill a quiet house or to accompany you on solo walks. We encourage you to pay attention to what kind of music feels good to listen to right now. Maybe you want something calm and easy to help create a pleasant atmosphere. Or maybe you want to be pumped up and encouraged by an upbeat tune. We've collected some of our favorite uplifting songs on our website *(beyondwidow.com)*. Listen to ours, or make your own. The right playlist can be like a good friend that you can turn to again and again.

Katharine Graham

A widow who rose to the occasion and helmed a major newspaper

Katharine Graham (1917–2001) was the publisher of the *Washington Post.*

Her father, Eugene Meyer, was a wealthy financier and newspaper-man who purchased the *Washington Post* in 1933 at a bankruptcy auction. Katharine had worked for a newspaper in San Francisco, and came to work at the *Post* in 1938. She married Philip Graham in 1940, and they had a daughter and three sons.

Her father handed over the leadership of the paper to Philip in 1946, and he took the helm. However, Philip's alcoholism, an affair, and mental illness culminated in his suicide in 1963. At that time, the newspaper world was dominated by men and Katharine commented later that it hadn't crossed her mind that her father might have viewed her as someone to lead the *Post*. Now the widowed Katharine faced a tough choice—either sell the paper or take on the job herself.

Katharine made the decision to become the first female publisher of a major American newspaper. She gained the respect of her male colleagues and was very successful in her new role, establishing the *Post* as a highly regarded publication in the newspaper world.

During her tenure, the *Post* and its reporters investigated the story which led to the publication of the infamous Watergate scandal in 1972. The *Post* was the only major newspaper to pursue the story. Katharine's courage was tested by threats made against her by

Attorney General John Mitchell if she went to publication. The *Post* did proceed to publish, which ultimately led to the downfall of President Richard Nixon.

As the women's movement gradually brought about changes in attitudes, Katharine worked to bring about gender equality in her company. She led the *Post* from 1963 to 1991 and the company became a media powerhouse. She proved herself as a gifted business executive and writer, winning the Pulitzer Prize in 1998 for her memoir *Personal History*.

Katharine's story is an inspiration to widows to make a leap of faith and take up the challenge of becoming the CEO in the next chapter of their lives.

"THIS IS GOING TO TAKE SOME
GETTING USED TO FOR BOTH OF US."

How to tell Lottie.

Patty

Your family and close friends need to be informed of your husband's demise… but here's a hard one: How do you tell the dog? Lottie, our old spaniel, was devoted to Richard.

After Richard's death, the first phase of change took its course, and life began to settle into a new routine. Lottie, Richard's faithful dog, was with me. She was a dog who had belonged to both of us, but she was certainly his BFF.

After a while I realized that Lottie was a widow, too. Her health had been in decline for a while. When she had Richard, she could carry on, but once he was gone, her spark gradually faded. I tried to comfort her, but she'd search his haunts in the den, sit by his chair, walk to his car, wait for him in the kitchen. She just wanted to be with her buddy, and sadly, she died eleven months after Richard. A precious link with my husband was gone and it was heart-wrenching.

Eating alone is no picnic.

Patty

When living alone with grief, eating regularly and by yourself can be daunting at first. Eating and preparing meals might be the last thing you feel like doing right now. But fueling your body can make you feel grounded, and a bit more stable mentally as well.

Here are some of my simple tricks to nurture my body with easy-to-prepare foods one can usually have on hand. And some tips on how to approach eating out.

AT HOME

– Keep a half dozen hard-boiled eggs in the fridge for instant protein. No mess or fuss and a good quick fuel.

– Have some prewashed lettuce at home, so you can grab a handful and toss it up in a bowl with some seeds or nuts and a precooked protein.

– Tapas are the perfect small meal: marinated olives, some slices of meat or cheese, cherry tomatoes or roasted peppers, and some nuts. Try an Aperol Spritz with it; that works really well.

– Have good crackers or crispbread at home; easy to keep and not like a whole loaf that will spoil halfway through. Pita bread keeps well also. It can be thrown in the toaster and will taste freshly made in no time.

– Smoked salmon is a good protein on a sandwich or salad.

– Costco has lots of single-serve hummus or guacamole, just the right amount for one person so a whole container won't spoil before it's eaten.

– Variety may be the spice of life, but sometimes you might want to eat the same thing over and over. If you find two or three things that taste good to you, feel free to just repeat those things until you feel like branching out.

– Remember… popcorn and a glass of wine can be dinner, too.

OUT AND ABOUT

– If you are out and about during the day, have lunch as your big meal of the day. You'll have other people around you so that you're not eating alone.

– Don't be shy. When you go out to eat, do what you want to do! If you want to sit at the bar and chat with the bartender, go for it. If you want to sit alone and read the news on your phone, that's just fine. If you don't want a huge meal and just want to enjoy an appetizer and a dessert, you do you.

– If you are invited to go out to eat with a couple (or if you'd like to invite a couple out yourself) and you feel like the third wheel, just keep in mind that your companions don't feel that way.

Disclaimer: These are general ideas from us for your inspiration. If you have special health needs or food allergies, of course contact your doctor or a professional nutritionist first.

"DO YOU HAVE A TABLE FOR ONE WITH MEMORIES OF BEING TWO BUT IS WORKING ON BECOMING COMFORTABLE WITH BEING ONE AGAIN?"

The search for solid sleep.

Patty

When widows gather, a common topic is the difficulty of sleeping. Sleeping may prove challenging at first, but rest is essential to restore body and mind. I had slept with Richard beside me for forty years. I knew my side of the bed and we had our routine that was solidly locked in, no matter what we had done during the day. I'd get into bed, often talking nonstop about some crisis in the day. We'd lay down, then he'd pat my hand and say: "Now, Patty Ann, quiet down! That'll get solved tomorrow. Right now, we need to get some sleep!"

In the morning, we'd wake up to his old clock radio blasting out the traffic report—a certain bridge was always backed up for twenty miles! No classical music, no quiet or solace or anything soothing like that. After the traffic report, we'd even listen to the sports scores that he might have missed the night before.

Do you know, I miss all of that! And it has taken me months to learn to fall asleep. It definitely gets better with time, but I also decided to redecorate the bedroom to help the process. I chose new bed linens and curtains. Richard had to have the room dark, so we slept in a tomb, with blackout shades, shutters and drapes. I like to wake up in the morning with the sun, so I removed all that paraphernalia and now have simple decorative shades, much more my style.

But most importantly, I redefined the real estate of the bed. I sleep in the middle now, because then there is no "my side" and "his side," and I find it spacious and comforting. I've made the bedroom a real "me zone" with my favorite music and my books all around me.

Fear.

Patty

When your husband dies suddenly, you become a different person immediately, with no preparation, no manual. You were a pair… now you are a singleton. That has profound effects on everything.

Fear is that feeling of terror which can suddenly overtake you. If you have children, you have lost your backup when it comes to those responsibilities! It's just you now. You are accountable for yourself and for them. You have lost a friend, a lover, a partner. Beyond that, in a lot of cases, he was the primary earner. In today's world, most women work, but it is often a secondary income. Women generally represent the primary caregiver for the family and run the home. Not any more! Now you do it all. That takes money, time, and stamina. Suddenly you have just one salary, so it's twice the work with half the pay. Now that can be really frightening!

I discovered there is no magic wand that rids us of fear. But it is reassuring to know that panic attacks don't last forever. Make yourself aware of the basic facts about fighting fear. Read up on it and learn some breathing exercises.

If fear looms really large and starts to overwhelm you, it is vital to SEEK HELP. So find a counselor you can lean on as soon as possible. It is important to remember that fear is something we all experience. Conquering fear can make you stronger. Building your tolerance and your confidence for handling it can feel empowering.

For those who are a birth mother, can you remember the fear you felt the first time you were left with a newborn with no practice of coping with a tiny baby? A little human depending totally on you… and you didn't even know how to put a stroller together! Babies don't arrive with their own manuals or guide books either. But you learned to do it and conquered that fear, one step at a time. Just like that, as I've coped with the loss of my husband, I've learned to face fears that once seemed insurmountable… one step at a time.

The numbers 59 and 75 to ward off pity.

Tesha

Fifty-nine and seventy-five. When you first come to know the significance of these numbers, they are shocking. But with further consideration, they make sense. I became a widow at forty-nine. The tsunami of support that came rushing in was rooted not only in dismay over the specific and tragic loss of my husband Keith, but also in the misfortune of becoming a widow so young. And the truth is, becoming a widow at forty-nine is young. The average age that a woman becomes a widow is fifty-nine. Not seventy-nine… fifty-nine. Furthermore, seventy-five percent of all wives become widows.

So why do these numbers often shock women when I share them? And why does having these numbers at my disposal feel like a weapon to ward off pity?

So often I have either felt or actually had women who are wives distinguish themselves from me. As if somehow they've figured out how to keep their husbands alive in a way that I couldn't. I don't wish for them to suffer the loss that I am going through. It is an awful experience that I wish we all could avoid. But I no longer live with the privilege of behaving with the belief that we just choose to avoid it.

I have reflected upon the saying that "misery loves company" with brutal honesty. For the first time in my life, I hear the saying in a new way. Perhaps the company that misery wants is not that others are going through the same awful experience or bad feelings, but that others don't distance themselves from the possibility that they could. That instead of wives saying to me, "I could never suffer what you are experiencing," they acknowledge that in fact they could, and that they are not better than me because they haven't had to (yet).

I have arrived at this part of a wife's journey earlier than most; that is true. But this does not make me one to pity or distance oneself from. Not me nor my sisterhood of 11 million widows. We have purpose and value and much left to do in addition to the "mourning" that will bring a new dawn.

I'm finding it hard to sleep in the house.

Tesha

When you figure out how you get your best sleep, I find it's good to set up those conditions as often as you can. Is it the time of day? A particular room in your home? Having people near to you or your favorite pet (real or stuffed) next to you? Sleep, when it comes each night, is a blessing. But hours beforehand I start to dread the inevitable time when I must call it a day and face that quiet twilight time before sleep takes over. My body fuels me with a slow gush of energy, convincing me each evening that, with just a few extra hours, I will get so much closer to the bottom of my to-do list.

It took several weeks for me to catch what was happening with my body's sleep avoidance. Now I know that my body was protecting me from what I dreaded most, the end of another day. My sleep avoidance didn't feel like procrastination; actually, quite the opposite. It felt like power in my ability to get things done. It felt like I was tapping into a deep well of strength that I didn't even know dwelt within me. But this pattern is not healthy, and if I'm not careful, it will have lasting damage. So how will I find sleep? How will I find comfort in the quiet of a home that won't make noise without me?

"THERE'S NO NEED TO PLAY THE WIDOW CARD, MA'AM. I'D BE GLAD TO BRING YOU MORE BREAD."

The widow card.

Patty

Occasionally, a widow can find herself in a tricky situation—such as trying to cancel a subscription for those overpriced sports channels that now nobody watches. To meet the challenge, it's good to have a few prepared phrases in your back pocket. Don't be afraid to use "the widow card"; it will stop 'em dead in their tracks!

"There's a new sheriff in town." Perfect for people who are asking for time or money.

"I'm a damsel in distress." Helps when something requires lifting or moving, or when something has stopped working. (I know I am not a helpless woman, but it is definitely useful to pull out this phrase occasionally.)

"You cannot be serious!" Great for someone asking something outrageous (it should be delivered quietly and seriously).

"Hm… that simply makes no sense to me."

"I hear what you are saying… but I really can't go along with that."

Don't abdicate.

Patty

Don't abdicate or become a shadow of your former self… you've got a lot more living to do!

Life may seem to be on hold immediately after the death of your spouse, but it shouldn't stop there.

The British Monarch, Queen Victoria (1819–1901), was an example of what not to do when widowhood comes. Following the death of her husband, Prince Albert, in 1861, she spent her remaining almost forty years of life in mourning. Compare Victoria with Iris Apfel, one of our widows featured in our "Wonder Widows" stories. Iris is a modern-day American designer and fashion icon who was born in 1921. She has reached her century and is certainly one to inspire us! Complete with her zany glasses, colorful clothes and beads, Iris entreats us not to be afraid but to "Be Bold!" As a mere seventy-something myself, I aim to be like her when I grow up!

Queen Victoria

A widow who used her power to protect other widows from death due to traditions

Queen Victoria (1819–1901), was nicknamed "The Widow of Windsor."

Victoria became monarch of Great Britain and its dominions at eighteen years of age. She was soon to marry her cousin, Prince Albert, in what appeared to be a marriage of love, something quite rare for her time and stature in society. Over the years, with their growing brood of children, they became the model of family life for the empire.

Victoria was widowed suddenly in 1861 at the age of forty-two years when her husband Albert died of typhoid fever. She went into deep mourning and virtually disappeared from public life, choosing to spend most of her thirty-nine years of widowhood in seclusion.

One can't help but wonder how differently things might have turned out for her, had she received the right help and advice, or perhaps the kind of mental health care as we know it today.

Victoria's life story has been retold in many films and documentaries but there is a little known way in which she was inspired to help other widows.

In 1877, Victoria was proclaimed Empress of India. When it came to her attention that widows in some parts of India were consigned to the funeral pyre along with their dead husband, she took action to outlaw that practice, known as "suttee."

Worldwide, India has the largest widow population with over 46 million widows recorded in 2015. Their plight today still ranks among the worst in the world; society there accords them little worth or compassion. For these widows, life is an unending struggle for existence.

How to support a widow.

By all

We know it can be hard to find the right words to say to someone who just lost their life partner. Their world is inside out and they will never be the same. But please don't let your own fear of saying or doing the wrong thing paralyze you. Here are some tips from widows:

- Reach out! A text will do. We'd rather hear "the wrong thing" than be ghosted.

- Take on a chore. One of my neighbors told her husband that he must take my garbage cans to the curb each week now. They know that my husband used to do this. He takes this role very seriously, and I appreciate it very much.

- Do not call her for expert advice about loss or tragedies that occur. It is OK to bring up the topic of her own loss, with care.

- Invite her, even if everyone else is coupled. Let her decide if she's up for that.

- Offer to help her with a project that's on her plate.

- Instead of saying "sorry for your loss," mention a brief, nice memory about her loved one. Share a nice sentiment, something only you can provide, rather than a phrase she's heard hundreds of times.

- Remember her birthday, and note her important dates on your calendar.

- Offer invites for coffee or a casual dinner.

- Suggest ways you might help rather than asking how you can help.

- Simply say, "Saw this and thought of you," or take over something that reminds you of her. It can be as simple as a flower in a pot, or one for her garden.

- Don't assume…

- Take her car to get washed.

- Give her a breakfast in a box.

- Ask if you can plant some flowers for her in her yard.

- Walk her dog, with or without her.

- Any and all help with Christmas trees. Buying the tree, untangling lights, getting it to stand straight in the stand.

- Get her a manicure. That is a gift for so many reasons (quiet, pampering, easy).

- Ask if she needs anything to go to cleaners or the post office.

- If she has children, offer to sit sometimes so that she can go out to dinner or to a movie.

- Show up, and keep showing up. In the immediate aftermath of loss, she may have lots of support. Show up then, but also in three, six, twelve months.

- Let her know she's not forgotten, through your actions and your words.

Who's your Patty?

Tesha

"You're going to be alright!" she quipped towards the end of our long lunch. Looking back now, I realize I was present in front of her, but numb and doing my best to focus. Patty is a force of nature and if you get distracted by the whirlwind she creates when she enters into a conversation or a room, you may miss the best of who she is. Who she has come to be. I don't know why Patty reached out to me. Sure, she knew that I would need help, but how did she know that I would need her?

In just a year now, she has given me so much. Of course, this includes welcoming me into her home to celebrate and rest. But that's not what I'm thinking of. You see, Patty has given me the opportunity to become an author. She has given me the platform to have a voice when I could have easily decided to turn inward. Instead, she reached out and said, "Let the world see you shine." She used the pain and wisdom of her own journey to make mine bearable. She saved Christmas and my birthday by offering her "heaven on earth" home to celebrate in the best way possible, on the ocean with loved ones and no busy agenda.

She gave me career advice and answered any question I was willing to ask. And she showed me sisterhood and friendship in the emails, texts and calls that we have shared over this year. She has seen me when I felt invisible in a year of overwhelming challenges. She has shown me that the choice to be a widow who thrives is not selfish and doesn't need to be rare.

But it might take a Patty—a person brought into your life to get you through. A person who is willing to let you see them, so that you can find yourself. Every widow should have a Patty. Not just a friend, but a friend who knows your journey and is willing to go for the ride anyway. If you're fortunate enough to have a Patty, don't let another moment pass without letting her know!

Picking up the Pieces

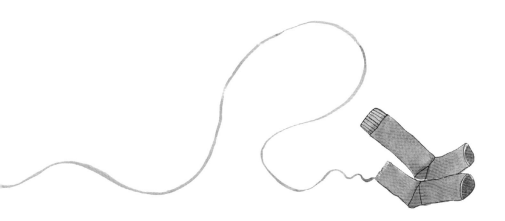

We do not know the journey, only
ourselves, and that is enough
to traverse the path.

—Anonymous

The big house clean.

Patty

Months passed and I felt I was living in a minefield. With every drawer and every cabinet I opened, there was a silent dread: his keys, his phone, his rain jacket, his tennis racket, his medications… the list went on and on.

I am not a big cleaner in the best of circumstances and this was certainly not the best of circumstances. But finally, it was time. The Big House Clean.

I started in the closet, and I told myself I would do thirty minutes a day. That was about what I could handle. My friend helped me to figure out where I could donate many of the things I certainly did not need anymore. Donating to the Salvation Army or the Army Veterans felt so much better than simply throwing things out, because Richard's things could have another life. I boxed up some pieces of memories. I wanted to cherish the good times they represented, but not make my house into a shrine or let it stay trapped in time. I threw out broken but treasured gear that Richard had put aside to repair and pairs of pants that he had kept for when he lost weight and could get into them again.

There were the crazy things he had bought, always with the saying: "You just don't know when you might need them." Things like… almost one hundred pairs of glasses… seventy-three baseball hats bought over time because of a color, cause, school, vacation… the lawn mower that was "just in case" we needed the lawn to look perfect in the middle of the week between gardener visits… the four sets of battery chargers because, every time we needed one, we could not find the last charger we had bought… the four Christmas tree stands for the variety of tree trunks we had dealt with over the years… and the tangled sets of Christmas tree lights… the cleaning and washing paraphernalia for the car, a chore we had not done ourselves in twenty years…

Some of the goodbyes were funny, some were poignant. Some were cumbersome and messy, but all of it needed to find a new home. In changing the house from "our house" to "my house," the treasures moved on. Parting with Richard's collection of size 38 pants was funny, and there were lots of clothes that he was planning to go back to once he lost weight. Whoever got those, got almost never worn clothes. Parting with his favorite camel cashmere coat took me two years to achieve. I remember him wearing it and his comment every time he did so: "This does look so good. George Clooney is jealous!" Actually, he did look wonderful in it, and knowing I wouldn't see that again was hard.

"YOU HAVE YOUR WIDOW
EMERGENCY KIT. I HAVE MINE."

Some thoughts on finances.

Patty

Money can be such a daunting thought for a widow. Not only have you lost your husband, you have also lost his income and in today's world two incomes are the norm. Often, a husband's earnings represent sixty percent or more of the family income and finance is an area he has dealt with. In many cases, women care for the family and run the home while providing a valuable secondary income. Now it's all down to you.

All this comes at a time when you are probably least prepared or able to cope with it, but there's no escaping this change. Mortgage payments, tax obligations, children's expenses, car payments, etc., need to be made despite your situation. The bills loom large and the world offers little sympathy for your new situation. Sorting out your finances is one of the most necessary and practical factors in a widow's transition. It may require help from a professional financial advisor, a good book, or even better, a new network of people qualified to meet the challenge ahead. Try to arm yourself with facts and knowledge wherever you can. Talk to people about how they manage their money and find as much financial information that fits the individual situation you are in. Like it or not, money is the fuel that runs the engine!

To make a start on this subject and even in preparation before you see someone, here are a few simple steps you can take:

List everything you and your family need to live, write down a budget and then review it. Do the simple calculation—money coming in and money going out. (You might feel that you want to escape to your Widow Emergency Room at first, as this could seem scary, but you need to face it!) You may find some ways to save. Oftentimes with some planning and more awareness, some costs can be reduced.

Got bills you can't pay? Call the company and try to speak with a human being about your options. That can be challenging in our tech world, but persist. Explain your situation and offer to make adjusted payments.

Instead of hiring someone for certain practical tasks, ask for help from neighbors and friends instead. You would be surprised how happy people are to help. For example, I was not afraid to lean on friends for help with "boy" chores. I had lists of things for when family and friends came over, and chore after chore, the lists gradually got done! I saved on handymen expenses, and guess what? My helpers even came back!

A few more global thoughts on financial survival:

In the past, the only option for financial survival as a widow was to remarry. Thankfully, in today's world there are other options. But no matter if you are feeling up to throwing yourself into a new dating life sometime in the future, or if you think you may never want to get married again, do consider that your current state might be temporary. Depending on your personal situation, you could have a whole other life with someone in the future. Just something to consider. But of course, this is not something you can plan on.

Consider if a new career path that pays more money is a viable option. Finding a new career can be a great life opportunity for a widow. But finding a higher paying one might not be so easy.

Could a promotion in your present job be a possibility? Can you muster up your confidence and take on a bigger role? Assume the outlook that your job is no longer a job; it's a career path. Be assertive and ask. What is the worst that can happen? They can only say no.

Do you own a home that you could downsize from? Depending on the housing market you live in, you could consider selling the home and buying one you can afford to maintain more easily without being house poor. This could be a really tough one, especially if you have children living with you. But your family will survive it emotionally, and it's better than feeling the constant threat of living a life beyond one's means. When I divorced, I moved out of a lovely home that would have sucked up every bit of extra cash I could muster. I chose a smaller, far more affordable townhouse that left me money to afford bikes and a trip to Disneyland once a year, and going out to dinner occasionally.

These are only a few things for you to consider. It's vital to get your finances in good order. Money takes on an even greater meaning for a widow. You are taking ownership of your finances and taking on a new role in being the CEO of your family or in your life. Talk and walk and find out what other women have done. Be assertive. Be your own advocatc.

(Find additional resources on our website at beyondwidow.com)

Eliza Hamilton

A widow who turned grief into giving and preserved her husband's legacy

Eliza Hamilton (1757–1854) was born in New York as Elizabeth Schuyler. She was the daughter of General Philip Schuyler and his wife, Catherine. At around 22 years of age, Eliza met the charismatic Alexander Hamilton and they married in 1780. Hamilton drafted the U.S. Constitution in 1787 and became first Secretary to the U.S. Treasury in 1789 under President George Washington.

Eliza and Hamilton had eight children in all, but the eldest son, Philip was killed in 1801, fighting a duel to protect his father's name. Then Hamilton himself died in 1804, while fighting a duel. His death plunged the grief stricken Eliza into a dire financial situation. In order to meet her husband's debts, she had to auction off the family home, The Grange, which she occupied with their seven surviving children. Friends entered the bidding and purchased the property, then sold it back to Eliza at a sum which she was able to afford. Eliza struggled to make ends meet and to pay for the children's schooling, eventually downsizing to a smaller house in a poorer area, but refused to be bowed.

Despite the pain she felt at the revelation of her husband's year-long affair with Maria Reynolds during Washington's presidency, Eliza made the decision to preserve her husband's legacy. Hamilton, who had been born in the West Indies, was orphaned at thirteen years of age and had benefac-

tors pay for him to study in America. The widowed Eliza was inspired to work tirelessly to fund the first private orphanage in New York and to establish The Hamilton Free School for the children of poor families.

A widow for fifty years, Eliza survived into her nineties, recalling past events vividly and enjoying spirited conversation. Her husband's life has been portrayed in the hugely successful Broadway musical *Hamilton* but the fact that we know so much about them both is all down to Eliza.

Do I still snore?

Tesha

I think that I might snore really loudly… but I don't know for sure. I suppose I should record myself or sign up for a sleep study. I'm curious about this, but only more urgent stuff gets addressed these days. A sleep study would tell me if there's a problem and give me a list of what to do about it, but I don't want another list. I have lists already. Like the water I want to drink and the squats I want to do daily.

I'm not taking good care of my health through my food choices and physical activity. I luxuriate in calorie-filled treats, telling myself that the kindness of a sweet treat is exactly what I deserve. My appetite for nutrient-rich food has dissipated and vegetables rot in my refrigerator. It's not okay. There will be consequences. And today is another day where maybe, just maybe, I will find the strength to make the best choices for my health. Because I'm pretty sure I snore. And even though it's not keeping anyone awake, I should do what I can to make it stop.

Do not become
a captive of the past.
Let go and dare
to dream again.

—Anonymous

Twenty years and fifty feet.

Tesha

Our decision to get married came within a few weeks. I know this because we met in October. I had my last date with someone else on October 31, and by the end of November, we had Thanksgiving with our families. We didn't tell them what we had decided, but we very intentionally made introductions. At Christmas, we did this again and decided that they had all of the information that they needed to bless our union the next month when we announced our decision to be married.

If there were audible objections, I blocked them from my consciousness. I'm sure there were plenty of silent concerns and doubts held in the hearts and minds of those who knew us best and knew life better than we. But we didn't hear them and they had no place in the fairy tale that we were writing for ourselves and our future. At twenty-eight and thirty-seven, with graduate degrees, purchased homes, very promising careers and plenty of mutual attraction, we asked, "What reason do we have to wait?"

Well, life taught us why you might wait for an engagement, a wedding, and children. And while I could teach a class on why to wait now, I don't believe that there was a person or a string of words that would have convinced me to wait at that time. What we knew for sure was that together the next step of our journey was only ours to take. And now looking back, I have peace that, while it might not have been the ideal way to enter a marriage, it was ours and the only way our history could ever be told. We knew enough to make a really good choice in each other. The rest we would take on one moment at a time.

And so, nine months after meeting, we married. Nine months after that, we became parents. We married in our backyard on top of fresh grass that we planted with seeds only months before. Keith promised me the lawn would grow in time for our July nuptials. It was my first time living in a single-family home after a lifetime of doormen, elevators and upstairs neighbors. "Are you sure the grass will grow in time?" I asked him again and again. After weeks of not seeing much of anything, I asked again with tears in my eyes and what I can only imagine was a very pitiful look on my face. Why did we need to use seeds and not sod? I just didn't understand. He had an explanation. It was a sound one, but I had doubts.

But on July 7, we stood on plush green grass with our close family and friends gathered. They witnessed our wedding and celebrated with us. Any lingering doubts about our quick timing were deeply overshadowed that day by the hopes and dreams bursting inside of each of us. We each had what we longed for, our person to make a family. A family to make. And we did.

Our twenty-year journey was not easy. We learned that there were usually two ways to do just about anything, his and mine. We learned that each of us had wounds to heal and dreams to adjust. We learned that sometimes our words could create deep and unintended hurt that might take more time than we had to heal. And though our journey was not easy, it was full of so much to treasure. We built a family. A family with its own traditions and history that will forever be because we made it.

Keith died less than twelve weeks before our twentieth anniversary and seven months after my father. He died a week before we were planning to celebrate my father's birthday with a small memorial in our yard. Keith had been preparing the yard once again, after years of gophers ravaging the space and winning the war each year. But this time he was going all out to ensure that the gophers could not win. And this time he was using sod.

My last moments with Keith were in the early afternoon. I hung in my hammock, and he sat in a chair close by. We sat fifty feet from where we stood twenty years before vowing to be wed until death do us part. It is so unlikely to leave a spouse forever in almost the exact spot where you took on the title. Especially given the adventure of the twenty-year journey we had. This time, in our final moments together, there was no fresh grass, but freshly tilled soil awaiting the promise of sod. And by the time my dad's birthday came the next week, Keith was gone, but I stood on fresh grass because the sod had arrived and once again, he had delivered on his promise of a new lawn in time to celebrate.

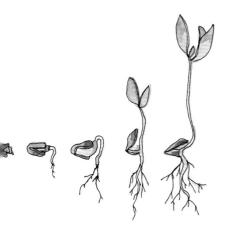

Keeping his spirit alive.

Patty

When that broken body no longer works for your buddy, he leaves it. But his spirit remains with you. Richard so loved his grandchildren that I knew he was leaving some of that spirit with them. I made it my mission to keep rekindling it in their souls. So I continue to buy the silly stuffed animals at Christmas that Richard bought them that sing silly songs. I pass out twenty dollar bills at unexpected times. I root for Michigan State every sports season even though it's not really my thing. And I celebrate his birthday with a party where they can bring a friend. I randomly email them pictures of Papa and them doing silly stuff. They laugh and tell each other their Papa stories, and this way his spirit continues. So whenever they come to a rough spot, they have the strong loving spirit of their Papa with them—my way of giving Richard a bit of immortality.

" WE ARE SO SORRY FOR YOUR LOSS. YOU HAVE OUR DEEPEST SYMPATHIES. UNTIL 5, THEN WE HAVE DINNER PLANS. "

Grief lasts longer than sympathy.

Patty

Isn't this the truth?! People just go back to their lives, while your life as a widow stands still… and as time goes on, they seem to expect you to get "over it" at one point.

Sympathy is an attempt at empathy, a person showing you that they are trying to understand what you are going through. And that's all well and good at the time of loss. But people need to understand that grief can last a long time. There is no real cutoff point.

As a widow, you almost have to rewrite the story of your changed life to try to come to terms with it as it is now. You have to begin to imagine a new narrative for yourself, so that the past does not turn into an out-of-control monster that takes over and ambushes you when you least expect it. It's not a closure point one will reach. It's not a choice between grief or living but learning to live with your grief. Once you learn to accept that, it becomes less pervasive, less of a monster breathing down your neck. It can soften and might change over time. You will find more agency.

To friends, loved ones, and acquaintances of widows… it is very hard to know from the outside at what stage of this process a widow might be, but please know that it is a forever process, not a magical endpoint.

To those who loved him first.

Tesha

You should know that she needs you, the widow. She may be too proud to ask. Or she may not believe that she deserves you at all. But she needs you to remember her. So try finding her from time to time.

She still has all that she had and is all that she ever was. Only more now. But it counts less because the truth is that the prize she gets for keeping the promise and for standing at the finish line is pity and the distinction of being the one person in the room no one wants to be.

But my friend, that is a choice and not a given. Just as in divorce, it never has to be ugly, even if it always has to be a devastating disappointment. What if we chose to revere the ones who remained to the end? The one who is all that is left. What if we applauded her and made sure she never wants for anything again? Who would we be then? Can we even fathom a society that reveres the widow? It would not seem wasteful to find wonder in the widow. Until then, I will continue to choose what is wonderful for myself.

Coretta Scott King

A widow who used her voice to fight for social change

Coretta Scott King (1927–2006) was an American author, activist, civil rights leader, and the wife of Dr. Martin Luther King, Jr. The two met in Boston while both were students. Coretta attended the New England Conservatory of Music and studied concert singing, while Martin was studying theology at Boston University. They were married in 1953 and had four children, Martin Luther King III, Yolanda, Bernice, and Dexter King.

The Civil Rights Movement began in 1954 with the *Brown v. the Board of Education* case, which ended segregation in public schools. When Rosa Parks refused to give up her seat to a white man aboard a bus in Montgomery, Alabama in 1955, Martin had been appointed as Minister of the local Baptist Church the year before. He organized a bus boycott and launched protests across the South and emerged as the principal leader of the movement, making his famous "I Have a Dream" speech in Washington, DC, in 1963.

Coretta and Martin dedicated their lives to social change but many threats were made against them. Their house was bombed in 1956 and King was stabbed in 1958. In 1968, her husband was assassinated. Coretta had been the main parent in their children's lives, but now took on the demanding role of sole parent. Although the King's marriage was marred by Martin's extramarital affairs, the widowed Coretta renewed the fight for the causes she and he had always believed in. She also lobbied for the institution of Martin Luther King Day in America, which is a public holiday on the third Monday of January each year. She continued protesting, speaking, and writing, and spent her remaining years campaigning strongly in America and South Africa to end all forms of discrimination. Coretta died following a stroke in 2006. She is known as the First Lady of the Civil Rights Movement.

Grief ambush.

Patty

Two-and-a-half years after Richard's death, I feel steady; I'm reasonably balanced, intellectually understanding his death and then… out of nowhere, something hits me! I'm in line in the coffee shop with a fellow that worked with Richard years ago. As we chat, he says: "I need to get him over for the final four. That man knows his basketball!" Suddenly, I'm back in the world of Richard alive. I simply burst into tears, say Richard has died, and run to the car.

I call it a grief ambush. No one means to hurt you, but it sometimes jumps out at you… a long-lost friend, a box of his favorite popcorn on the grocery shelves, his barbecue sauce at the back of the cupboard. (How did that not get thrown out?) I'm not sure where the coping skills are to handle these moments; certainly, running out of the coffee shop in tears was embarrassing at some level. Oh well. I try to think of those times as Richard moments that I put away in my secret "Why I love you" compartment. Sometimes that works. Other times, I just turn away and tear up. That's the nature of a grief ambush.

Passing time.

Patty

I was looking online at Salvador Dali's great masterpiece: *The Persistence of Memory.* That's the one with the melting clocks. This surreal piece of art so expresses the strange sense that time takes on when your mate has died. Minutes can drag on for hours, and a lifespan of memories can seem to go by in seconds. Some memories feel so strong, and others seem fleeting, as if they had barely happened. One minute you can feel your husband just stepped out the door for an errand, and the next minute you can feel he and your former life with him all happened far away in the past. And everything can be distorted.

Whatever
you want to do,
do it now.

There are only
so many
tomorrows.

—Pope Paul VI

The gift of time.

Patty

One thing is for sure… as a widow, my husband's departure has given me time that I now have more control over. However, without plans or intentions to re-purpose your life, time can hang heavy and gradually become your enemy. I try to look at the free time I now have as a gift. I regard time as a friend in my new life, that allows me to do more of the things I want to do. I loved my husband, but he consumed a lot of time!

A bike lives on.

I love biking. And because I loved it, Richard biked—but not as often, not as far and not with quite as much enthusiasm. I understood that, so to help him, I got him an electric bike which he grew to really enjoy. When he died, I left it in the garage for two years. I was in a real quandary. What was I to do with it?

Then I went on a biking trip with Richard's wonderful life-long friend, Bob Snyder. Bob was still riding the bike that Richard had passed on to him twenty-eight years previously. New England folk are notoriously frugal! I suddenly thought, "Time for Bob to have a new bike!" I know the spirit of Richard is in that bike. It was a lot of work to get the bike back to Massachusetts and no small price for shipping, but it was a perfect gift to Bob from Richard.

"THE LONELINESS WAS HARD AT FIRST, BUT ONCE I FOUND THE SNORING APP IT WAS LIKE HE NEVER LEFT."

Black widow.

Tesha

I wasn't raised to wait for a prince to save me. I was raised to save myself and to help others as soon and as often as I can. I was raised to protect my heart by choosing my mate well and making sure that I had enough skill to make it on my own, should I need to. The women in my family worked outside of their homes and educated themselves above the norm to ensure that they would always have a way forward. Most of them were also wives who nurtured their marriages and their children and passed down generations of progress. There is such a woman called a Black widow who does not prey on serial spouses but builds a legacy of family rooted in love, pride, loyalty, and strength, despite the obstacles that have come to her and her family.

In the United States, marriage was illegal for enslaved people and so it wasn't until 1866 when most African Americans could legally marry. It took another 101 years to make interracial marriage legal through the *Loving v. Virginia* decision. My family has been in the U.S. for centuries, but for most of that time was not able to fully participate in the American dream. This included recognition of marriages protected by the state. The interracial union of my maternal grandfather's parents was well before their time, though his nearly-white skin belied the success of the strict segregation of his birthplace in Virginia. So perhaps this is why the term "black widow" was usurped by the widely known murderous term. But now that I've joined the ranks of the Black widow, I implore you to celebrate her. She has love to give. She has been groomed to take care of herself and others. She has seen deep pain and survived. She is determined to not be done.

There are a hundred
paths through the world
that are easier than
loving.

But, who wants easier?

—Mary Oliver

Where's the hammer?

Patty

When I became a widow, all sorts of changes were forced upon me: the ownership of houses, cars, investments, taxes… and the list goes on and on. I decided to take things one at a time with the motto JUST DO IT, and check it off the list. Eventually they all get done, and nobody is keeping a scorecard.

In addition to the big responsibilities that are now solely mine, there are all the little things that used to be "boy jobs," like trash going out, car trouble, internet glitches, pest control, lifting heavy boxes, climbing ladders, roof repairs, heating, ventilation and air-conditioning, in-law connections. These don't stop and wait while one grieves. So I had to tell myself, you either just do them the best way you can, or just get help!

I recently ventured into the "boy zone," the garage! I was searching for a hammer because I've been rehanging pictures. I know now where all the tools are. Yesterday, I even replaced the car license plates with new ones. That deserves an award! It took me forty-five minutes to find the right tools (a Phillips-head screwdriver and proper bolts) and figure it out, but now I know that I can do this.

Today, I replaced the toilet seat! I undid the screws of the broken seat, went to the hardware store, and bought a new toilet seat to replace it. Well, my friend Jayna was here with me. She actually reads directions and follows them and that's a big help! We replaced the seat and I now know what a wrench does! That was a small triumph!

"OH, HI - I WAS JUST MAKING THE BED."

Getting to know your neighborhood resources.

Patty

I'll pass on a handy hint here that works for me. If you need an electrician, painter, roofer, etc., rather than searching online, just walk or bike around the neighborhood and see where the work trucks are. If it's not a dire emergency, I find the interaction with other human beings works much better. Stop, introduce yourself, and see if the worker has time, or knows someone that can help. These workers know the neighborhood and have usually worked for at least one other neighbor. They know how to get things done in your area!

Johanna van Gogh

A widow who captured the attention of the art world and championed her family's legacy

Can you imagine the world of art without the paintings of Vincent van Gogh? The brushstrokes of this agitated soul conveyed energy and life onto his canvases, giving us such wonderful paintings as *The Starry Night, Irises* and *Sunflowers*? The fact that the works of this Post-Impressionist painter came to the attention of the art world was due solely to the tireless efforts of Vincent's sister-in-law, Johanna (Jo) van Gogh (1862-1925). She was the woman who ensured Vincent van Gogh's genius was recognized.

Jo's marriage to Vincent's younger brother, Theo, an art dealer based in Paris, catapulted her from a steady existence as a teacher of English in Amsterdam, to the capital of France with its artists, theaters, and street cafés.

Vincent figured largely in the lives of the young couple. Theo strove to promote Vincent's work, and their home was soon filled with a regular supply of his paintings, but few attracted buyers. Jo and Theo cared for and supported Vincent through his periods of poor mental health, and even named their baby son after him.

Barely two years after her marriage, Jo's life changed dramatically; Vincent, at 37 years of age, had shot himself, while her husband, Theo, aged 33 and in failing health, died a few months later. Jo was suddenly alone with a young baby and around four hundred of Vincent's canvases. Jo returned to Holland and opened a boarding house, which gave her a home and an income to support herself and the baby. She made the decision to take all of Vincent's paintings with her and hung them around her house, certain that her brother-in-law's work, long dismissed by the critics, would be appreciated by the art world one day. She put aside time to read the host of letters the brothers had exchanged and realized that Vincent's writings all described the deep emotions behind his paintings.

Armed with that knowledge and the paintings, and fired with enthusiasm, Jo gradually won over Van Gogh's critics. Gaining in confidence, she took Vincent's work to exhibitions in galleries and museums around Europe. In 1905, she arranged the largest ever exhibition of his work, with some 484 canvases, at the Stedelijk Museum in Amsterdam.

In an art world dominated by men, the courage and determination of the widowed Jo van Gogh finally ensured the acclaim that Vincent's work so richly deserved.

It is my choice now.

Tesha

For me, the shift from married life happened in an instant. Two decades of shared groceries and calendars and bedsheets and dreams. I didn't realize the shift right away, perhaps because of the constant activity that lasted for several weeks after Keith's death. There was so much to do, and we had so many friends and family around. They helped to plan meals and memorials and where to place the sea of flowers that arrived throughout each day. Eventually, and as is appropriate, we left their constant thoughts and they moved on knowing that we would be OK.

Quickly came the new reality that the choices were mine now. All of them. I don't feel equipped to make every decision, to sign every document, to represent both of us. My decisions are not just based on my heart's desire, but I listen quietly for memories that would direct me to Keith's heart, too. At times I have approached others with vulnerability to ask for the generosity of their opinions.

Many of my choices will fall short. I have already forgiven myself for this. My heart's hope is that I will be OK with the disappointment that I may bring to others. That muscle is new and will take much practice.

Building a new mantra.

Patty

Several generations of our English friends came over for Richard's celebration of life party. Amongst them was David, who is never one to miss a party. He came with reverence and respect to honor a man who has always been in his life and always made him laugh. When he returned home, David wrote me a note which said:

"Well, I'm not sure if it was the 36 holes of golf, the total lack of sleep, the hundreds of people or the gallons of alcohol we drank, but it feels like I am returning from another planet. I have learned something huge from this event. Having reflected on Richard's life, I am now looking at my own life in a different way. And when I come to a decision, I think: 'WWDD—What Would Dick Do?'"

I read that and said to myself, "And that's exactly what you are going to do, Patty Ann!" So now, when I'm starting to twirl in my head, I take a big breath and I think "WWDD." Thank you, David, for a unique and marvelous mantra!

His walk, my climb.

Tesha

Keith's last heart attack was not his first. After the first one, he committed to strict eating and took his medication religiously. During the pandemic, he choreographed a six-mile walk through our neighborhood and town that he did each morning for nearly a year, always at 5:45 a.m. Rising well before dawn and wearing a hoodie, he marched silently past homes with sleeping families and pets and dreams. This was not just exercise; it was a risk-taking act of defiance for his daughters and for me and for himself. As a six-foot Black man living in a town that is one percent Black, his daily routine was a regular taunt of a neighborhood he had resided in for more than two decades but never really called home. Not in his heart, anyway. He felt the neighborhood hadn't really embraced him the way he had experienced in Tennessee or Mississippi, where he had spent his formative years.

On the day Keith died, we did his walk together, as we had come to do many, many days in the months before he passed. And two days after his death, I did every step of the walk alone. I didn't feel alone. I felt his steady presence pushing me up the hills, and I ran into some of the regulars that he saw each day. Every step I took was an act of new defiance in the face of unimaginable pain and uncertainty. But just as he had done so many times, I made it, too. That walk will always be his, and the journey I continue to take, ours.

Just in case you need a stamp.

Patty

Some time ago, the post office started selling rather lovely, artful stamps with pictures of dinosaurs, baseball players, hearts, airplanes. They were called commemorative stamps. Richard did not have a stamp collection, nor did he send out many letters in the mail. I'm not sure why, or when, or where Richard started buying these commemorative stamps, but he had hundreds of them. They popped up in all of his three desks, in drawers, in glove compartments in the car. "You just don't know when you're going to need a stamp," he'd say.

As far as I know, he never actually used any of them. Perhaps they were his art collection. Many are really beautiful. They all have different values—32, 36, 43 cents. It's like a bingo game to actually use them. You often need a 1, 2 or 4 cent stamp to bring them up to the cost of the present-day postage. He was far too frugal to put two 32 cent stamps on an envelope when all he needed was a 32 and a 4 cent stamp. To put 64 cents on a letter was a big waste of money!

I'm determined to use up his stamps, although he sits on my shoulder, whispering, "You only have two Babe Ruth stamps left. Careful, one of these days, those could be really valuable!" I do have the 2, 3, and 5 cent stamps to add to them to respect Richard's policy of not wasting one of these precious stamps. Now the phone company, the Visa folks, the PG&E Company all get these colorful stamps on their bill payments. I'm sure whoever opens the Internal Revenue Service mail is curious as to why they are getting a dinosaur with an additional 3 cent stamp.

If you remember or discover some special quirk or other strange habit your mate had latched onto, hopefully you can laugh or shake your head and say: "Yes, that certainly was my husband!" and enjoy a beautiful moment of connection.

The inherited garden.

Patty

Richard found our Palo Alto home and bought it while I was away on a trip to Europe with my mom for one week. I had been gone just four days when he called to say he'd bought a house, but we didn't have to take it if I didn't like it… obviously, I realized this man could not be left on his own!

Luckily, the house was gorgeous and I loved it. Richard had fallen in love with its amazing English garden. He just adored that garden. He spent hours thinking about it. He planted and trimmed and enjoyed every minute he spent there. I was not a "hands-on" gardener and was oblivious to much of what was happening. I got to enjoy the garden, but as a spectator. I learned to expect a spectacular garden, until he left.

When Richard died, I suddenly inherited the responsibility for the garden. While I was no gardener, much was in place and I thought all I had to do was to maintain it. Think again! There were decisions to be made. The once-magnificent 150-year-old oak tree was diagnosed as dying; I would have to orchestrate its removal and a regeneration project. Again, I was faced with losing a part of Richard with the loss of this old tree, which he loved and which was an iconic part of our street. It was tragic to witness its demise; the whole neighborhood was in mourning as it was removed.

As I got to know the garden more deeply, I realized I needed to keep track of the seasons and the trimming and the replanting. I had regarded it as outdoor housekeeping, but soon I was magically converted. A garden is a space-time machine; although it's intangible, it is transformative. I began to grow hope. I got excited with sprouting seeds. The garden had real life dimensions. Birth, growing, blooming and death all happen regularly. With time, I began to look at the garden as another gift from Richard to me. He left me a blueprint and structure to connect with beauty and nature. It is the gift that just keeps giving. I truly appreciate that, Richard. Thank you.

And so I continued to grow into my role as the person in charge of the garden. One day I read about the widow iris. That flower spoke to me—a black flower—so different. Yes, I knew I wanted some of those! The widow iris has thin, angular leaves and from these, emerge amazing, sweet-scented blooms. The flowers, which appear in spring, are almost fluorescent green in color, with black velvet petals.

Flowers have their own history and story. I'm starting to add my story to this garden.

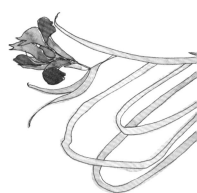

Harriet Wilson

A widow who captured her world in a novel and raised awareness of the difficulties African-Americans were facing in the 19th century

Harriet E. Wilson (1825–1900) was born to an Irish washerwoman and a barrel maker of African-American descent. The young Harriet experienced a life of hardship early on. Her father died when she was little, and her mother left her on a farm, where she was indentured as a servant until she was eighteen—not an uncommon arrangement then for orphaned or abandoned children. In return for their labor, they received room and board and some schooling or training.

At age eighteen, Harriet began working as a house servant and seamstress. In 1851, she married Thomas Wilson, who purported to be an escaped slave and travelled around New England giving lectures about his life. However, Harriet, pregnant and ill, was abandoned when her husband went to sea. She was sent to the Hillsborough County Poor Farm, and it was there that her son, George Mason Wilson, was born in 1852. Her husband died in 1853, aboard the sloop Cabassa in Cuba.

Harriet was now a widow with a baby and was destitute. She returned her son to the Poor Farm, unable to make a living to support them both. While working in Boston, she wrote *Our Nig* and copyrighted it. It was published anonymously in 1859. Her aim, which she recorded in the preface, was to raise money to help her sick child. We can only imagine the hours she spent toiling over her manuscript when her daily duties were done; her delight when it was published; and then her anguish, just months later, when her little son died of a fever.

For a few years, Harriet seemed to disappear, although it is recorded that she remarried. She was mentioned regularly in *Banner of Light*, a Spiritualist publication, as a medium and active member of that community. Sustained by faith, she gave lectures on healing, labor reform, education, and her life experiences, often adding humorous commentary.

Although Harriet was born as a free Black, her book compares the "freedom" of a Northern servant and a Southern slave. In her book, the heroine, Frado, experiences cruelty and overwork at the hands of her mistress, Mrs. Bellmont—the "she-devil" in Harriet's tale, which has its foundations in Harriet's own childhood and adolescence. *Our Nig* was Harriet's only known book, but it raised awareness of the racism which existed in the North in her time. Her novel is a testament to her determination to remain unbowed in the face of many challenges, including widowhood, and is now acknowledged as the earliest published novel by an African-American in North America.

I live alone now.

Tesha

I have one school year to figure it all out. That's the limit I have given to myself and others. By the end of that year, I need to have worked out the next steps in my new life—a life on my own. I know better than to think that time alone will heal all. Of my nearly fifty years, I've only spent two of them as a sole occupant of my dwelling. Yep, other than that, I've had parents, a sibling, roommates, a spouse for two decades, and now my children. But my kids will and should move on and move out. I have a year to solve this puzzle; if I don't, my children will worry and delay their own progress. I can't have that.

I couldn't part with Bucky.

Patty

My husband, Richard, had a neck roll he called Bucky. My daughter had a blankie, my son had Bozo… and Richard had Bucky. The kids outgrew their must-have sleeping items, but my six-foot, 245-pound husband did not. He had Bucky for over 20 years and Bucky went to bed with him every night. Nobody knew this but me.

One time, Richard accidentally left Bucky behind in a London Hotel. As soon as he realized he'd forgotten to pack Bucky, Richard called the hotel and was hugely relieved to know he was still there. His friend John drove twenty miles to get him and then mailed Bucky to us in California. Richard was sixty-two at the time…

As I began the widow's task of sorting through my husband's clothes, athletic gear, and everything else, there was Bucky! Getting things to go where Richard's spirit could follow was one thing, but figuring out what to do with Bucky was something else. I knew I just couldn't part with him and he ended up in my bottom drawer. I don't sleep with Bucky, and he makes the velveteen rabbit sitting beside the bed look positively cavalier, but I still have him! The kids will find him one day. I wonder if they'll remember how comforting Bucky was to Richard. They can choose whether to throw him out. I can't.

"I'M USED TO HIM BEING HERE WHEN I'M HAVING SEX."

Stuck in my dress.

Tesha

This week I led a school, a company, a household and a nonprofit board. It's a lot. I am a lot. And it is really all good. Today alone I've toured one of the country's most successful and innovative animal shelters, reconvened with a national leadership group, met with a New York-based book agent, planned a diversity presentation with a friend I used to only know as a fan from afar and watched two performances of a musical production by the girls at the school I'm running this year. It's a lot, and even the hard parts are good. The good parts are great. I pinch myself knowing how fortunate I am.

But of course, it's not all good. And there are moments that still take my breath away. But I don't look for those moments. I'm not hiding from them. I let them come when they arrive. And sometimes they come because things that used to come easily with his help are no longer happening. Some of them are no longer possible. Those are the moments that take my breath away. The solutions are disappointing and leave me without a real fix. They only get me through.

Tonight, after arriving home at 9 p.m., at the close of a very full day, I sat on my bed and reached around to unzip the emerald green dress I wore all day to celebrate the opening of the musical *Shrek* at my school. I reached behind and couldn't grasp the top of my zipper. It was so far out of reach. Now, I've learned that with enough of my effort, I can get out of this dress eventually. I'm getting used to this familiar feeling of being stuck until I gather my focus and strength to make my way out. Again. It's particularly difficult when the thing that is creating the challenge used to be so, so simple. So simple that I don't even remember it happening most times. Good Lord, how many times did that man help me in and out of my dress?! Less than ten seconds to suit up or unplug.

And so I choose to lay here a little longer. Gathering my strength, taking a breath. So that I can reach further up my back than is possible at first try. Then maybe I can finally relax into this night.

Missing the power of two.

Patty

Whatever you do to keep your day-to-day life busy, there will always be those times that pop up to haunt you. Times when you miss your buddy sharing a meal and discussing your day with you, his presence at family gatherings on holidays, going on vacation as a couple, his warmth and measured breathing at night.

A dear friend of mine said to me: "I miss Joe and I miss my life with Joe." Those are two separate issues and I had not thought of that before. The status of a couple, as Richard and I were, was quite powerful in a way. We were the life of the party. We traveled with friends, enjoyed going to the theater together, held fund-raisers, and relentlessly cheered our grandkids on at sports games together. The list goes on. I still do some of the same things, but what has vanished is a sense of power and confidence that comes from being a couple or a strong team.

One widow said to me, "It will never be the same without him." That was depressing! But then I thought about it. Everybody dies. Seventy-five percent of married women become widows. We know as a couple we will die, but rarely do we die at the same time. In my case, if one of us had to die, I think it was better that Richard went first. He would have been completely overwhelmed with what was left of his life after the funeral.

I know he would have remarried in less than thirty days. He loved casseroles and hated taxes. I may have been the love of his life, but let's be practical—he had to eat and he wasn't going to do taxes!

So, although life without Richard won't be the same, it will be OK. I am committed to making this next chapter of my life an exciting, vibrant course of fresh experiences and connecting with new people. I am not going to be sitting in God's Waiting Room for my time… I have places to go, people to see, and new challenges to meet!

Mindfulness.

Developing mindfulness is a necessity when so many decisions are made solo and they come at you hard and fast. I must admit, this state of mind has never been my strength and I have had to actively work on finding it and developing it. I am much more a quick-draw, immediate action, spontaneous person, so this approach took real discipline for me to develop. Honestly, for me, it was one of the good things that came out of the pandemic. Time slowed down. I was alone in a big house. I had to be quiet and think. That was a new concept for me!

When I make myself quiet down and breathe deeply, I find it lessens stress, dampens self-doubt, and allows me to focus my attention where I need it. This is absolutely the best mind-body medicine you can give yourself, but it is not easy.

By taking more time and being mindful, I began to really taste my food. I biked and saw all sorts of shades of green. The quiet in the air was eerie at first, and then magical. My circle of people was still small. I appreciated every visit and I think I learned to listen to them far more.

I gave up the "hurry" in my life, at least at times. I savored different activities in different sections of the house. By taking time to go through my closet, for example, I found out I did not need nearly as many clothes as I previously thought.

In reading about mindfulness, I learned that medically, it does have positive and dramatic results on your brain and blood pressure. I am sure this is a virtue for everyone, but for a widow newly doing so many things alone, with lots of big and small decisions to make, this becomes a real necessity. Maybe you're like me and you've been hearing people tout the benefits of mindfulness and meditation for years, but you think you don't have the time and interest to give it a chance. Take it from me, an Irish whirlwind who loves action and motion… mindfulness really merits the discipline and work it takes to develop and practice it. Do give it a try!

I'll always have a piece of the Royals—and Richard.

Patty

There, in the corner of the shower I never use, I spotted a bottle of Penhaligon's Blenheim Bouquet Men's Shampoo, partially full! In case you are not familiar, it's the fanciest shampoo a man can own. Seeing the bottle reminded me that Richard discovered this brand in London. He loved that this shampoo was used by the royals. He bragged about it all the time, as if he and the royal princes— William, Harry and (then) Charles—all met together at the hairdresser's to get their hair washed with Blenheim Bouquet… and now, I had some of it!

I felt sad when I used the last drop, then I thought… wait a minute, I can buy this when I'm in London and keep that tradition alive and in place! I find it great fun to know I can have an endless supply of his favorite shampoo, "as used by the royals" he would always say whenever he reached for it!

My children may never read this book and when they're doing my cleaning out, they'll find that shampoo. They'll be curious about where that fancy bottle of shampoo came from. I like the idea of tantalizing them… if they don't read the book, they don't deserve to know how it has appeared as a staple in my life!

On your last day.

Tesha

The dash in my company name (Joy-Raising) is intentional. It's a reminder of Linda Ellis's *The Dash Poem*, which is a reminder that we don't control the year we are born or the year that we die, but only the dash that falls in between on our headstone. And by control, it is to say that we have choices. What will you do with your dash, the poem asks. I think I've been interested in this question because of the brushes that I've had with my own mortality and because of the heart attack that Keith had several years before he passed. His heart attack put us on notice. And the blood clot in my lungs and passing out and breaking my ankle, put us on notice. Today, and maybe not even all of it, is all that we have.

I have so much peace that Keith's last day was a really good one for him and for us. The fact that he didn't know it was coming or suffer for very long is likely what he would have preferred. He'd taken the COVID-19 pandemic lockdown very seriously, and as a family we spent more time together that first year in the pandemic than we had in so, so many years. I promise you, we never took two-hour morning walks regularly before then. Or had lunch at home together with our teenage daughters on school days. Or listened to music on vinyl and painted and did puzzles. It wasn't all roses, but it was all meaningful. And he submitted to this slow pace with grace and appreciation. I've described his last day several times. I spent so much of it with him and that feels like an honor to witness someone's last day. It was simple and calm. A nice walk with his wife. A nice drive with his daughter. A nice meal with his wife in her favorite hammock in the backyard where we were wed. A nice goodbye that wasn't meant to be forever.

I wonder if the strength and confidence that I have found within myself was always there. Was it waiting to be called upon or has it developed in these moments since? I don't know that the answer matters. I'm scared. But I know what I'm scared of and I'm trying to address it. That feels more useful than denying it or inaction. I let myself feel all that I can. So that I know that I am still here.

Football's promise of a first-and-10.

Tesha

Today I'm watching my first Super Bowl in over 20 years without my built-in expert to rely on. I didn't know what a first down was when I met him, but over time, I learned. I like to say it was osmosis. We watched the game so differently. He was somehow able to put words in the mouths of commentators; they always seemed to parrot exactly what he said only seconds before.

Eventually I became a fan, often making loud outbursts after big plays and asking lots of questions. It took forever for me to understand what a first down was, and thereby the anatomy of a drive down the field. I didn't know what I didn't know and I didn't know how to ask to understand. But somehow, I figured it out. Whether at your own 10-yard line or at first-and-goal, your possibilities are as full as they will ever be when you are at a first-and-10. And in only 10 yards, you get to have that feeling again. It was all that I needed to understand about the game to become curious enough to want to learn more. And in time, I did.

For us, the Super Bowl often included a big trip either to the event itself, or to Vegas or somewhere he could enjoy the game with buddies during a multiday celebration. By us, I mean he went, and I pouted. When the Super Bowl came to Levi's Stadium where our local team, the 49ers, play I knew for sure it would be my first time being able to attend. And Beyoncé herself was the headliner for the halftime show! But it wasn't to be. Instead, after waiting until the day before the game to finally commit to buying tickets for the girls and me, he left us in the parking lot on game day and attended without us when one of his clients showed up with only one ticket. I never understood that choice or let him live it down. For years, I used the incident to punctuate our arguments. It was a visceral memory and just seemed so clearly wrong. I argued that I passed up many opportunities to secure tickets on my own but had relied on him to make it happen. I could have done better for myself but I chose to rely on him. Sure, I was disappointed in him, but I was mostly disappointed in myself for being vulnerable unnecessarily.

Today, watching the Super Bowl without him after spending all day sorting through his tools and supplies, I had new clarity which also felt similar to regret. You see, there were many tools, gadgets, and supplies that I couldn't identify. All this time I could have spent learning to fix a house. But I didn't. Now it is up to me to figure it out. And what else could he have taught me? Moments like these are painful. They can come quickly and make me light-headed. Rather than becoming overwhelmed, I try to grasp for the lesson—the lemonade, the way out. Today what saved me was grasping for and holding appreciation for my journey to football through him. I am grateful for the mastery I feel when

I watch a game now. I looked over his many tools that I laid out before me and felt genuine excitement for the journey to learn and master them, just like I did his game. I'll learn from him, and not with him, this time. I'll wonder what project prompted the purchase of each tool and I'll imagine how tickled and proud he is knowing that somehow we will continue to build together. First-and-10 again and again.

Barbara Sonneborn

A widow who brought us the stories of widows from both sides of a war

Meet Barbara Sonneborn (1944–present), born in Chicago, acclaimed artist, film creator, photographer, and children's author. On January 1, 1968, Barbara's husband Jeff Gurvitz had departed to fight in Vietnam. Just eight weeks later, he crawled out of a foxhole and was hit by a mortar. On her twenty-fourth birthday, she received an unexpected letter: "We regret to inform… your husband has been killed at war in Vietnam."

At that moment, Barbara faced a very different future. Grief, sadness and loss were catapulted into her life. She was a war widow.

It took Barbara ten years to begin her film *Regret to Inform* and another ten years to complete it. The project became a mission and helped her to survive by turning her grief into positive action. Not only would this be a gift of love to her husband Jeff so that his life was not wasted, it would also show war in a way that had not been seen before. Barbara was determined that people should see face-to-face the tragedy and futility of war and learn to respect the humanity of others.

To make the film a reality, Barbara had to overcome many hurdles. Although there were support groups for American veterans, she was not aware of any similar networks for the forgotten army of widows left behind. She undertook mailshots, contacted veterans, the children of widows and the press, and discovered some two hundred war widows. She listened to their stories and was overwhelmed by the suffering the war had inflicted upon them.

Barbara embarked on a journey through Vietnam, photographing and interviewing people to show the sorrows of war and the pain of a beautiful country being torn apart. With the help of Xuan Ngoc Nguyen, who acted as her translator, she looked at her own grief as well as that of four other widows from the Vietnam War. Barbara's film portrayed the senselessness of war as American and Vietnamese widows told their moving stories and united in a call to end war.

Sonneborn's beautiful and impactful film rewarded her with many accolades, including a Sundance Film Festival Award.

Beyond the finish line.

Tesha

"What's next for the widow?" A passive thought that few truly ponder. What's next is her own demise, whenever it finally comes. What's between now and next for the widow matters to few it seems. She no longer belongs to anyone. She has lost the comfort and legal status of being a wife. This is not an indictment; it is an observation of all of us. What is her commitment now? And what is our commitment to her? Anything that we do now is an act of kindness and grace. She is not ours. She was his. And he is gone. So what is her point now? If he leaves her with a lot, does it truly become hers? Or is it always still his? Is she always still his?

These are the questions that I ponder now. Not often enough to find answers, but often enough to know that the story remains incomplete. You should know that she needs you, the widow. She may be too proud to ask. Or she may not believe that she deserves you at all. But she needs you to remember her. She needs you to try finding her from time to time. She still has all that she had and is all that she ever was. Only more now because of what she has endured.

Finding a New Path

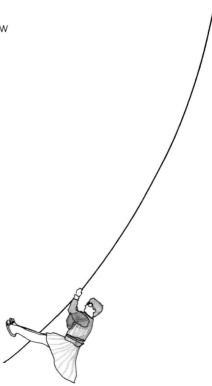

Once you choose hope,
Anything is possible.

— Christopher Reeve

All we have is now.

Patty

The past is the past and you cannot turn the clock back. Nor can you magically return to how it felt to be single before marriage. You have the memories of your youth, your marriage, and a rich inner fabric, but you are in different territory—the territory of NOW. The future is unpredictable but the present is fertile ground for an evolving you. Don't waste it! Just keep moving.

When I am asked how my own life is evolving after widowhood, I can truly say that my first venture into authorship, by way of a children's book, has enabled me to create ideas, meet new friends and discover new resources, all of which have been incredibly life-enriching. So I tend to agree with Albert Einstein when he said:

> Life is like riding a bicycle,
> To keep your balance,
> You must keep moving!

The ring trilogy.

Patty

One day I looked down at the ring on my finger and twisted it around. What does one do with their wedding band after their husband has passed? How long is one expected to wear it? My ring was relatively new. The story of wedding rings had been a bit of a comedy for us because we each had more than one. When we got married, Richard had insisted on rings, but consistently lost his. Overall he had three different ones. His rings seemed to follow the same road as his keys and his phone… always in a state of perpetual loss. I was married to Richard for forty years and spent three of those years looking for his keys!

When Richard died, I asked some friends who were widows what they had decided to do with their rings. My friend Joan said: "I knew that the marriage contract had promised 'till death do us part'. But I didn't feel 'parted.' My husband was no longer there in person but he was part of me. Only years after his passing, I decided we no longer needed the rings. He was in Heaven living a new life and I knew I would join him one day. I took the rings off and put them in my safety deposit box. I occasionally need to visit the box to retrieve some papers or other items and I look at those rings. They were worn through good times and bad. They announced our love to the world. I often wonder what will happen to them when I die but the children will do with them whatever they wish."

My friend Judy took a different approach and said: "A friend of my husband's worked as a jewelry designer. He offered to take my wedding ring and Ray's wedding ring and put them together. He melted the gold from both rings together, added the stones I had, and now the two rings live on forever as one."

In the end, I decided to do something special to include Richard's last wedding ring, and my idea was linked to a lovely memory we had shared. Whenever we traveled Richard always picked up a little rock or pebble to take home as a keepsake. On our first trip to Japan, Richard gave me a small rock from the shore of the Sea of Japan. "This is for our fortieth anniversary," he said. I teased him, saying, "I'm getting a rock, huh?!" He smiled and replied, "Yes, indeed. Something really different."

A couple of months after he died, I found the little rock and came up with my idea. I took the rock, along with a recut diamond from a previous wedding ring of mine, to a jewelry maker. We designed a wonderful artistic ring together, which included both the rock and the diamond mounted on Richard's last wedding ring.

I love it and I now know exactly where his ring is… it's on my finger and I get to wear it every day!

The Widow meets the Hobbits

Time and memories.

Tesha

I wish that culturally I had more support through this process because I have no clue what I'm doing. Two-and-a-half months in and I continue to take one step at a time in my new identity. Sometimes I wish I could wear a big "W" on my chest so people would know to be gentle with me. To offer me an extra dose of grace. Because some moments I'm right there, and then there are times when I'm in a memory. In a moment I'll never have again. Usually, a moment that I would do over if I could. And that's the weight. None of it can be done over. It is our history. Our truth. An impact on my "now." Sometimes I'm not in the moment or in the past, but in a future that I know is only a possibility, a suggestion without absolute probability. No guarantee to hold on to. Sometimes the future looks dark, and I see myself as a small part of a world that forgot to bring me with it. But mostly, I see a future where I am vibrant and engaged in the moment as it is presented. I've learned that I cannot depend on much beyond my faith. And I've learned that my faith can move mountains.

Louise Penny

A widow who found the courage to start writing again

Louise Penny (1958–present) was born in 1958 in Toronto, Canada. Louise loved reading mysteries as a child. But she built a successful career in broadcasting, and in 1994, met her husband, Dr. Michael Whitehead. She confided to him her wish to try writing mystery novels, which he supported wholeheartedly.

For nearly five years, her attempts at writing came to nothing until she began a mystery novel. She centered it on a character named Armand Gamache, who was inspired by Michael. Her first book, *Still Life*, was finally published in 2005. After rejections from many publishers, it received critical acclaim and became a bestseller.

Some years later, Michael was diagnosed with dementia. Louise faced that diagnosis with courage and cared for him throughout the progress of that condition. Michael died peacefully at home in late 2016, at the age of eighty-two.

Louise was now a widow and doubted that she would be able to go on writing. She and Michael were a devoted couple and he had always been her inspiration for Gamache. Now he was gone and it was a struggle for Louise to just get out of bed every morning.

Some months later, Louise found herself at the table where she always wrote. Over three days, she found the courage to write a single sentence. She began a new book, *Kingdom of the Blind*, and was filled with happiness to discover that she could continue to write. Michael had not been left behind.

Find the simplest change you can,
and then make it.
Wake up tomorrow,
and do it again.

—Brianna Wiest

Little things are my wins.

Tesha

I'm finding it's all those little things that can get to me… and together they become a big issue. With my "First Responder" suddenly gone, there's no honey for the "honey do" list. Like garbage man, mechanic, driver or grill master.

There's just me and my willingness to try, or ask for help, or go without.

And I have felt satisfaction in each of these choices as I made them. When I rebuilt our bed in a new room to make it mine, I felt great accomplishment because I tried and conquered what felt beyond reach. Each week I listen with gratitude as my neighbor wheels out my garbage bins to the curb offering me help because I need it. And when I show up again and again at events big and small without a plus-one in rooms full of couples, I feel strong to be enough on my own and curious and hopeful for the possibility of what could be.

Entertaining for widows.

Patty

There are lots of subtle reasons for a widow to entertain. It's a way to signal to people that you're ready to connect again and also get invitations. Conversations in one's home can be longer and more meaningful than at a restaurant. I would invite a couple or two, add a couple of widows and this makes for a diverse evening, with no one feeling like a fifth wheel. I would try to connect everyone and make them feel part of a group.

As a new single, a widow can take advantage of the different vibe and make things unusual but keep it simple. And most importantly, not a lot of work! You want to spend the time reconnecting, not catering. And nobody will expect you to be a gourmet chef, unless you always were one. But these events should allow you to widen as well as maintain your circle of friends. From my experience, people seem happy to be included and I have a good reason to get the house organized or decorated. Try it for yourself!

Until I create it.

Tesha

"The place in which I will fit will not exist until I create it." — James Baldwin

This quote is one of many in which he perfectly captured the beauty and pain of living life as a Black American. When I heard this quote recently, I didn't receive it through my lens as a fellow Black American but instead as a young widow. Now, I'm not a young woman, but I am a young widow. At forty-nine, I felt too young to fall into this category of people that I'd never thought much about. And now, at fifty, I sometimes feel terribly silly starting anew in so many ways. My peers are established and ready to continue their glorious ride into the sunset. I cringe when my thoughts dwell on how few social places have been created for "the widow."

In the quiet of my heart, I can imagine a culture that reveres the widow. Her home is fully paid and her children's financial needs are secured through adulthood. Soon arriving at her doorstep is a nutritionist, trainer, masseuse and spiritual guru. Her wardrobe and home are appointed with fresh beauty. Her dance card is full and a security system is installed to keep her from falling victim. Her car is maintained and she only drives it if she wants to. And she not only receives acts of kindness, but has the chance to place her love in an impactful way.

My life now exists to create this place for myself. No one wants to be a young widow. But we should all want to be our best selves no matter what path we are on. Amen.

Bridget Mulkern

*A widow who set out for a new country
to build a future for her family*

In addition to our stories of well-known women from history to inspire you, there are countless other widows, little known but brave women, whose lives and moments of decision are untold. In the process of putting together this book, we learned about the story of one such woman: Patty's great-grandmother, Bridget Mulkern. Patty had not been aware of her great-grandmother's story as a widow, and in learning about her, Patty added an ancestor to the community of widows she's built.

In 1894, Bridget Connelly Mulkern stood at the door of her humble abode on the tiny, windswept island of Inishlacken off the west coast of Ireland and made a huge decision. Bridget was forty years old, a widow with six children. Life on the island was an endless struggle but she could see one ray of hope— to go to America. The courage, determination, and the risk-taking required to make that decision were immeasurable, but she made it and forged a new path for the future generations of her family.

Bridget's decision meant dividing up her children. The older ones stayed behind with relatives while she and the two youngest children (the second to youngest being Jack, Patty's grandfather, then age fourteen), set sail for America and settled in Philadelphia. Bridget held fast to the belief that, in the land of opportunity, education, and freedom, there would be a better life for them.

In due course, Jack Mulkern

married and he and his wife had two children, one being Patty's mother Winifred. The family moved to California, where they thrived. Patty was inspired to trace her Irish roots and in June 2022, she visited Inishlacken and found the ruins of the house where Bridget had lived. Patty learned about her story and felt a kinship with this resilient widow whose brave choices had shaped the course of Patty's own life.

Patty's belief is that a widow, under all circumstances, needs a path. She has found widowhood hard, sometimes lonely, and always challenging. Yet when she stood on the rocks of Inishlacken, she knew that if her great-grandmother could do what she did, then she could also find her path.

Permission.

Patty

Maybe you are sitting on the fence about something. You think, "Should I do this?"

You want to go on that weekend trip to see that jazz group perform? Go! You want to buy the same tennis shoes as your seventeen-year-old granddaughter? Do it! You're going to a wedding and you want to look outrageously gorgeous but you wonder if it's too soon after your loss? Buy the outfit and get your makeup done!

Who are you waiting for to give you permission? Do you need permission? Permission granted! Go for it. Be bold. Be playful. Be wicked!

The accessory of a ring.

Tesha

The truth is that I didn't have to decide to remove my ring. I hadn't worn it regularly for a few years. It was the feminist in me. I wouldn't wear mine if he wouldn't wear his own. It took me a few years after he took his off for me to actually do this. I thought not wearing it would scare him into putting his back on. It did not. I saw it as an act of revolution because in our professional and social arenas every woman wore her ring. At least, that's what I told myself.

After Keith died, I saw people noticing that I wasn't wearing my ring. This quick glance again and again felt like so much judgment. I haven't worn my ring in five years! Has anyone noticed before now? When I wear it occasionally now, I wear his wedding band as well. It honors the history that we made together. On days that feel particularly hard, when the world feels particularly big, wearing our rings brings me some sense of belonging and grounding. Is this silly? A false sense of comfort? Not wearing the ring in protest when he was alive was not meant to be a sign that I wasn't married. Wearing the ring now is not a false declaration that I am still married. I am not. When I wear our rings now I wear them as a single woman who is connecting with her former status of being married and the husband that made it so.

"LEAVING MY WEDDING RING ON AFTER
HE DIED IS PARTLY A SIGN OF MY DEVOTION
AND PARTLY A SIGN THAT IT'S STUCK."

You are the captain of your ship.

Patty

Beneath dark, gathering clouds on a late November afternoon in London, Marian and I hurried toward a street corner, intent on hailing a taxi to take us back to the hotel where our family was staying. Our attention was suddenly drawn to a long corridor of light visible in an elegant gallery. We paused and peered inside. At the end of that pathway, against a stark, white wall, stood a powerful piece of modern art, a steel sculpture finished in matte black. A female form. A woman alone.

She drew us toward her, two solitary visitors taking refuge from the coming storm, as if she meant to send her message to us alone. She seemed to be standing tall above the bow of a ship, directing its course. No matter that she already had a title, *Mobile l'Australienne*. She was made by the French artist and designer Philippe Hiquily (1925–2013), renowned for his Surrealist works.

In that moment, we both recognized her as the symbol of the widow…
the captain of her own ship!

Consider finding a new career.

Patty

If you become a widow at the stage of your life where you are in the full swing of your career, or you have to work due to necessity or financial constraint, then this might not be a talking point for you. Let's face it: not everybody has the luxury to ask themselves what they are passionate about when they have to meet deadlines or put food on the table. But if you are a widow who strongly feels it's now or never, then this is your time to follow a new curiosity or passion for something… don't hesitate to go for it! You can find yourself a new career any time you want.

I was married once before, and my divorce was devastating, financially and emotionally. When forced to consider a new career path after my divorce, I thought about practicalities as I made my choice. I met Richard when he was thirty-one—a young, unencumbered, lovely man—and I was thirty-four with two children, aged seven and ten. Marrying me was a lot for him to take on. I was recently divorced and determined to find a new footing for my life. I had to support two children and I needed a career that paid well. So, my criteria were as follows:

1. Don't worry about titles (you've got kids).
2. Get a job not involving travel (you've got kids).
3. Find something to sell without a moving part (you're not good at fixing things).

Commercial real estate caught my eye and it fit my criteria. I didn't know how realtors got paid, but I knew it was good money. I searched for an opportunity and got hired. Now I was newly married with a new career, and so that marvelous chapter "Married with kids and a career" had begun! I couldn't have known it then, but I went on to have a vibrant and successful career in commercial real estate for many years to come.

When facing a major life change, it can feel daunting to try on a new identity or career. But don't be afraid to follow your gut instincts, your skills, the practicalities you need to meet and your interests. You only live once, so go out there and find your opportunities. You got this!

A very special message.

Patty

There is one thing, even two years after Richard's death, that I have not changed and that's the answer message on our home phone. I suspect that men often record this particular message. I know that's what happened at our home. It's still his message and I'm sure I'm not alone in keeping it. I tell myself people who call need to think there's a man in the house. But, deep down I know it's because when I miss Richard, I can call the house and hear his voice. It brings me great comfort and pleasure.

Let's talk about sex, baby.

Tesha

Or maybe let's not. Talking about sex can feel a bit taboo in any context and it's no different for the widow. Likely worse. It somehow seems wrong to think about it, most particularly when your husband has passed away not too long ago. You are in new terrain. But that doesn't mean you can't get some clarity for yourself.

The good news is decisions about sex are all your own. And they are all right! Don't wait for permission; it won't come. The world won't give you a collective green light to have pleasure again. Instead, ask yourself what you want in this new stage of your life. And then take a few steps towards it and ask yourself again. Things can feel familiar and completely new all at the same time, and that's ok. What's most important is that you own your journey and embrace what your heart tells you... or your body, in this case.

Don't miss the magic of this moment.

Tesha

Now is always present, if we just let it be.
It's too busy with itself to manage our regret.
And it finds it only ridiculous to join us in
worrying about our future.
It's ready, always.
Available is its constant state.
The sooner that we see it, the more of it we have.

Now is the culmination of all that ever was.
It has never paused or hurried.
It invites us to see everything.
Just as it is.
Every last drop.
Just as it should be.

In his garden.

Patty

It was late July and almost two years since Richard's passing. In a few days' time, I was hosting a party in the garden, which would be filled with friends and family, including our grandchildren, to celebrate his life. His beloved garden—my husband's pride and joy—looked wonderful thanks to our gardener Kim, who had assisted him (and now me) over many years with its care and development. In preparation for the party, Kim had made sure the garden was "Dick Bush proud and ready."

She was doing a final walk through to check that everything looked its best for the coming event. She paused by the dogwood tree, one of the last big things that Richard had wanted planted. These trees normally bloom in the early springtime, but this one was blooming in July. Growing up through the tree was a beautiful delphinium; just how it arrived there, we don't know. It certainly wasn't planted on purpose, but now, here it was, with its beautiful blue flowers announcing its presence. I looked up the meaning of the delphinium, and found the following:

> "Delphiniums symbolize cheerfulness, goodwill and protection.
> They are used to communicate encouragement and joy, as well as remembering loved ones who have passed."

How about that!

The party was a great success. A fleeting glance towards the clusters of people there that afternoon suddenly rekindled memories and made it so easy to believe he was there somewhere amongst them, sharing one of his great stories. I feel certain Richard still is in that garden sometimes.

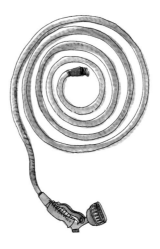

Georgia O'Keeffe

A widow who fought anxiety and made masterpieces in her artistic oasis

Georgia Totto O'Keeffe (1887–1986), was born in Wisconsin in a time when few women received recognition as artists. She knew from age twelve that she wanted to paint. She attended art school, although what she was being taught there didn't really seem relevant to her. However, in 1912, Georgia discovered the work of artist Arthur Wesley Dow. His style made a deep impression on her and helped to confirm her future path as an artist.

Georgia's paintings attracted the attention of Alfred Stieglitz, a photographer and the well-connected owner of a New York gallery. He introduced her to Duncan Philips, a champion of American artists, and her career flourished. Thanks to her paintings, she became a key figure in the American Modernism movement.

Although the marriage of Georgia and Stieglitz lasted from 1924 to his death in 1946, their story reminds us that not every marriage ending in widowhood is necessarily a happy one. Theirs was a union under strain. Alfred was attached to life on the East coast, while Georgia loved the wide vistas of the American West. He was overbearing, while she was of a nervous nature and had experienced breakdowns. After his death, Georgia settled his estate and dispersed his personal art collection to various museums. She was now alone, in her early sixties, a woman who had suffered from anxiety throughout her life yet hadn't let it hold her back from doing the things she wanted to do.

In 1949, Georgia summoned up her courage and made the decision to move permanently to New Mexico. She had a house at Ghost Ranch and a studio house in Abiquiú and was inspired by the bold beauty of the area. She lived very simply with her two dogs and devoted her time and resources to painting and creating her new life. Georgia guarded her privacy carefully, but was a prolific painter, giving the world an amazing art collection including her wonderful flower paintings. Her work reflected the area around her; instead of city skyscrapers, there were now beautiful landscapes, particularly Pedernal Mountain, which she painted some thirty times and regarded as her "private mountain." Throughout her life, exhibitions of her paintings attracted great attention and she received many honors. Georgia's story highlights the importance of retaining a keen interest in life—a vital element in a widow's well-being.

Being inspired by grief.

Patty

Although our personal experience of loss can be daunting, it can—with time—also turn into a positive force and empower us to do amazing things. The loss of my husband inspired me to donate time and effort to benefit causes embraced by my local Rotary Club that Richard was really fond of. If you have the luxury of time, consider finding something to put your energy into that's dear to your heart. A cause such as research into cancer or heart disease, you name it. It could take the form of anything from a sponsored walk to volunteering some time to help in a local community project. Achieving a goal for a good cause is uplifting for everyone involved, and can make you feel part of something larger than yourself.

And sometimes the way to get inspired by your loss is to achieve new personal goals for yourself. Five laps at the local pool (becoming fitter and healthier) for example. Or be inspired to live the best life that you can with the cards you have been dealt. Wherever you may stand, it's good to have a project in the works. But a word of warning here—set small, achievable targets, especially at first. You can always increase these when you're ready; just don't plan to climb Mount Everest straight away! Trust me, I tried!

The unexpected widow.

Tesha

And somehow she managed
To find peace in a place
That hadn't even contemplated
Her existence.

Widow to wife.

Tesha

I've had thoughts round and round about this and I think that I've come to the correct conclusion that the only way to escape the status of being a widow is to become a wife. Again. Which of course is the only way to put yourself in the unfortunate position of where you might find yourself a widow once again. These are things that I didn't much contemplate before losing my husband, Keith. And my thoughts about it now are not urgent but consequential.

I remember telling him in a jovial conversation on this difficult topic that my expectation and desire would be for him to search and find someone to make him happy without any reservation if I were to go first. Perhaps because he didn't think we were mortal or because he expected to go first, he chuckled and said OK.

I do not know if I will go from widow to wife. At times, it is too much to contemplate. But the thought also brings flickers of hope. Picking a mate when you only know marriage in theory, seems much easier than making the choice with decades of experience. I know too much. It doesn't seem fair to ask someone to live up to the loss and expectations that I have developed over time. Most wives become widows, but most widows do not become wives. By choice? Circumstance? Because of undeclared expectations? What I know for sure is that wife is not the only way to be a woman. And I am learning that being a widow does not mean that I can no longer be a wife.

Living apart together.

Patty

So, as an older widow, what happens if you meet a man you are attracted to and you begin a new relationship? We don't lose our need for a healthy, loving, intimate relationship just because we are growing older!

However, if you and your new partner contemplate taking the relationship further and sharing a home, you (and your family) may have reservations about that next step. Here's a new twist to the "happily ever after" bit. More older singles who have begun new relationships are now opting not to move in together, choosing instead a way of life known as LAT, or living apart together.

If you're living in your own home, LAT is an option which can have mutual benefits for you and your partner, since it offers the chance for you both to maintain your own personal space while enjoying the benefits of your relationship together. It works for couples who live close by each other, enabling them to spend time together three, four, or more times a week (your bedroom or mine tonight?), and it can also work for couples who live further apart, where they perhaps spend their weekends and holidays together.

Thinking of moving in with your partner brings up many things to mull over, including finances, where you will live, possibly selling your home, and other compromises which may have to be made. Unless the new person in your life is some years younger than you, not least of the issues you need to face is that an older man is more likely to have or to develop physical health issues. If your new partner maintains his own space, current or future health problems allow his family to be able to share the care needs, or help with provision of care, rather than it all being down to you 24/7 (and vice versa if the situation arises).

During your marriage, you will have been the primary caregiver for many years for members of your family. Taking on that role again for a new partner as you grow older is a daunting task; sapping your time and energy to the detriment of your own health, and limiting opportunities to see your family and friends. If you are working, you may have to stop, or if you've developed new interests since widowhood, you may have to give these up. Living apart together enables both partners to offer love and assistance without being totally locked down.

As a new relationship develops and you consider moving in together, take a little time to consider what could work best for you both for a happy and fulfilling new chapter. Our best wishes go with you as you set out on your future path!

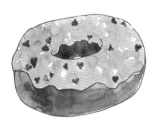

For the irreverent widow out there.

Patty

The holidays bring back a flood of memories, and a widow could quite easily end up on the edge of depression if she's not careful at this time of year. Now, I live in Silicon Valley… the land of innovative ideas! So, here's one irreverent, crazy idea that just might work, or at least is worth a try… why not "rent" a "husband" for the holidays?

Hear me out! Look up the app *Taskrabbit*. One can hire caterers, drivers, gardeners, errand runners, handymen. You can even hire a Santa! So why not hire a "husband"? Age, experience, education… all are flexible. No intimacy required. Someone with a built-in skill set for tasks during the most hectic month of the year. It just requires someone with the ability to follow directions without asking questions or complaining.

This person can...

- Get the tree in the tree holder so that it stands straight
- Untangle and hang Christmas lights
- Get the inflatable snowman from the attic, blow it up and put it onto the lawn
- Stuff Christmas cards, should you write any
- Stand in line at the post office to mail packages
- And the list goes on…

You get the idea? If suitable, he could even be your escort at Christmas parties! He could offer a set of working hands in a month of countless chores and would allow you to do just the tasks you want to do, without getting into an argument—in my case, getting the house decorated for entertaining. It would certainly lift your spirits and allow you to enjoy a time that is usually rich with joy, but also a roller coaster of emotions. At the least, you have company (even if you pay for it). And perhaps you'd even have fun along the way.

And if a particular "husband for hire" doesn't fit the bill, you can do something you can't do so easily with a real husband. You can always fire him! Maybe this outrageous, disruptive idea just might have some mileage to it!!

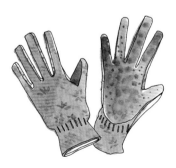

Iris Apfel

A widow who became an iconic style guru in her golden years

Iris Apfel (1921–present) is a modern-day wonder widow. This American businesswoman, interior designer, and fashion icon has packed a lot of living into one hundred years! With her huge tortoiseshell glasses, stunning outfits, and statement jewelry, there's no mistaking style guru Iris Apfel!

Born Iris Barrel in Queens, New York, from her earliest years Iris was fascinated with the texture, color, and pattern of fabric. After university, she worked for Women's Wear Daily and then as an interior designer. In 1950, she married Carl Apfel, the love of her life, and together they set up their renowned textile company *Old World Weavers*. Following her retirement at age eighty-three, Iris was thrust into a new life as a celebrity after The Metropolitan Museum of Art in New York staged an exhibition of her clothing in 2005, entitled *Rare Bird: The Irreverent Iris Apfel*. In 2014, she and Carl starred in the documentary *Iris* by Albert Maysles.

When Carl died in 2015, Iris could have just walked off into the sunset. However, she believed that even after becoming a widow at ninety-three years of age, you could still do amazing things! While realizing that life gets a little harder as you grow older, new experiences and new challenges keep it fresh. "You only have one trip," Iris famously once said. "You might as well enjoy it."

Iris was determined to make the most of this next chapter in her life. Becoming invisible was certainly not an option she considered! In 2016, she starred in a TV commercial for a French car and won the Women Together Special Award of the Year and the Women's Entrepreneurship Day Premier Award. In 2017, she appeared in the documentary *If You're Not in the Obit, Eat Breakfast!* Toymaker Mattel created a Barbie doll in her image in 2018. Iris is the oldest person ever to receive this accolade. She followed this up in 2019 by being signed as a model by IMG, at ninety-seven years of age. Now, at one hundred years young, Iris Apfel is a great example of a resilient and creative widow!

Living in the front row.

Tesha

Buying one single ticket for a performance is something that I've done regularly for a long time now. When I try to think deeply and remember the first few times that I did this or why, I can't find an exact moment or reason. About as close as I can come is that in high school I became used to having interests that were different from my friends. And even though it sometimes meant that I needed to take extra safety precautions because I attended events alone, the important thing was that I still stepped out of the comfort of being in a group in order to have the experience that I wanted.

Even as a wife, I continued to attend many events alone. Movies, theater, music concerts, museums, fundraising events, lots of things. It wasn't that I required it, but if it meant the difference between seeing the original cast of *Hamilton* on Broadway or not, the choice was wildly obvious to me. And so, even at times when I've wished for a plus-one, I've refused to stay home to avoid potential social awkwardness. Like the time that I showed up alone for a comedy show with open seating, and the ushers called one to the other through the room

"Only one!" It was like a game of telephone being used to usher me to my seat.

I have recently made a shift and seemed to have leveled up on my willingness to not only attend events alone, but to sit in the front row. This wasn't even a conscious trend at first, but now I regularly choose the front row if I can. And you know what? The seats are better! What I've discovered is that when you sit in the front row, you can choose to be oblivious to the rest of the audience if you want to. At a recent live music performance, I sat within ear and eyeshot of the musicians. I chose to experience their performance as if it were all for me. And why not? I am choosing to live life from this day forward without apology for the space that I take up. I feel ready to fully realize my power and voice and use them to advocate, teach and inspire. It doesn't make up for this awful loss. But it does give me much more to wake up for.

Your new identity.

Patty

Before being a widow, you probably had lots of titles: wife, homemaker, chef, gardener, community participant, parent, maybe grandparent. The list goes on. And maybe you were working in some capacity. When I became a widow, realization dawned on me: I was not just a widow; I was now an independent person, and for better or worse, in charge of all decisions. For most of us, after decades of marriage, that's a new viewpoint. At first, it is daunting, but it is also empowering.

Some titles will disappear, and many will have new, broader meanings. But YOU have the power to define the scope of those parts of your life and what those new titles are. You are now the CEO and chairperson of the board and it's your challenge to orchestrate what happens next. I would venture to guess that you'll find you were already doing much of the work anyway. But now you have the awareness and the power to run your life as you want it. Feel free to define your roles so that they fit into the next phase of your life.

I carry you with me, into the world.
Into the smell of the rain and the words
That dance between people.

And for me, it will always be this way,
Walking in the light, remembering
Being alive together.

—Brian Andreas

Contributors.

Patty McGuigan

Patty McGuigan became a widow in 2019, following the death of her beloved husband Richard, whose demise occurred a few weeks after the onset of his final illness. She has a long-standing successful career in commercial real estate in Silicon Valley. But she also always had another passion, making books of her travels that included sketches and stories of her adventures. Patty has raised two children and has four lively grandchildren. Seeking a new challenge during the early days of the COVID-19 pandemic years, Patty and co-grandmother Marian Lye from England decided to take up the endeavor of becoming co-authors. From across the pond they began writing books for children together, of which two are published.

Even though Patty was leading a busy life with all her projects and passions, she at one point realized that finding her new place in the world as a widow was more complex than just keeping busy. And when looking to books for guidance, she realized there was nothing out there that looked beyond the grief part of it all. But Patty intended to have a whole new chapter in her own life and was already thinking of writing the book that would become *Beyond Widow*.

At that point she met Tesha McCord Poe, the widow of a fellow associate in the real estate world, Keith Poe, who had died suddenly. They set up a lunch date and Tesha was immediately interested in this project. Patty welcomed a second voice for the book and so the collaboration with Tesha began.

Tesha McCord Poe

Tesha McCord Poe is an attorney turned law teacher, turned passionate nonprofit leader who has led fundraising efforts totaling more than $100 million. Tesha is the founder and CEO of Joy-Raising, a consultancy that partners with organizations to address their most critical fundraising and diversity/equity and inclusion (DEI) needs. Prior to founding Joy-Raising, Tesha spent more than a decade working as a senior administrator in independent schools in the Bay Area.

Tesha became a widow in 2021 when her husband of twenty years Keith passed away suddenly. She and her two teenage daughters were immediately surrounded by a tsunami of support from the community they had built as a family for two decades. This included a lunch with Patty, one of Keith's longtime colleagues whom Tesha had always admired as one of the only women in Silicon Valley commercial real estate. That fateful lunch resulted in a bond and sisterhood over their shared status as widows. They also shared an ambition to empower themselves and other widows with the way they chose to move forward in their lives. Tesha and Patty both have a passion for writing and believed their different perspectives, backgrounds and life stages would help women navigate their way through this experience. And *Beyond Widow* was born.

Marian Lye

Marian is an author who calls Weymouth, England, her home. She and her husband raised their three sons together, and she shares three wonderful grandchildren with Patty McGuigan, who all live in California. She published a World War II history book *Weymouth at War*, now in its second edition, and has co-authored two children's books together with Patty: *Leonardo and the Time Travelers* and *Leonardo's Magic Sketchbook*.

With her writing experience, Marian was the perfect partner to help us understand widowhood in different cultures and contexts, and offer a broader overview on widowhood. Having worked with Patty before, she was enthusiastic to join her and Tesha in the creation of this book. She reached back through the decades to find our "Wonder Widows," and provided research and writing support throughout the creation of this book.

Priska Wenger Mage

Priska is an illustrator and visual artist with a BA in illustration from her native Switzerland. She received a Masters of Fine Art at the City University of New York. Aside from her fine art work, Priska illustrates for books, advertisements, and magazines. She is a long-standing editorial illustrator for the Swiss magazine *Surprise*. The illustrations for *Beyond Widow* are handmade drawings in ink and watercolor on aquarelle paper.

After living in New York for a decade, Priska moved back to Switzerland with her family. She is a mother of two young boys and the wife of a musician with whom she collaborates on artistic projects. She loves gardening, restoring old furniture, and hiking in the wilderness of the Swiss Alps.

John Klossner

John is a cartoonist whose work has appeared in the *New Yorker*, the *Wall Street Journal*, *TIME*, *Reader's Digest*, and numerous other print and electronic publications around the globe.

John lives with his wife, children, dogs, and chickens in Maine, living the way life used to be.

Published in 2023 by McDorobush & Associates

Essays © 2023 Patty McGuigan and Tesha McCord Poe
Illustrations © 2023 Priska Wenger Mage
Cartoons © 2023 John Klossner
Historical contribution, research and editing by Marian Lye

ISBN: 979-8-218-14513-2
Printed in China

Creative direction, concept and design by Maria Mayer Feng
Design and editing by Kate Ryan for Studio Maria Mayer Feng, LLC
Cover design by Alison Forner

beyondwidow.com
@beyondwidow

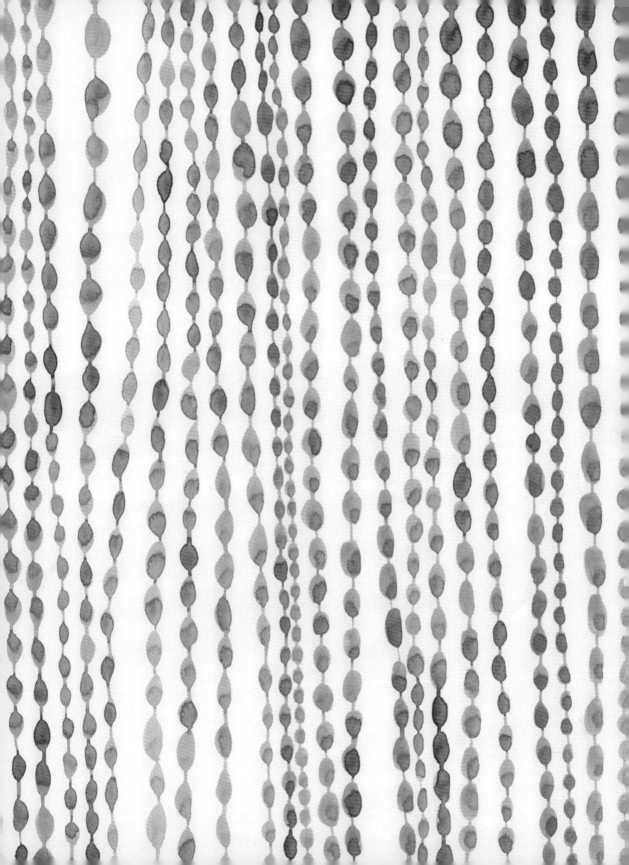